Mark Harrison

Grammar Spectrum 2

Pre-intermediate
With answers

Oxford University Press

Oxford University Press
Great Clarendon Street, Oxford OX2 6DP

Oxford New York
Athens Auckland Bangkok Bogotá Buenos Aires Cape Town
Chennai Dar es Salaam Delhi Florence Hong Kong Istanbul Karachi
Kolkata Kuala Lumpur Madrid Melbourne Mexico City Mumbai Nairobi
Paris São Paulo Shanghai Singapore Taipei Tokyo Toronto Warsaw

and associated companies in
Berlin Ibadan

Oxford and *Oxford English*
are trade marks of Oxford University Press

ISBN 0 19 431412 X (with answers)

© Oxford University Press 1995

First published 1995
Eighth impression 2001

No unauthorized photocopying

Illustrated by Ann Johns

Typeset in Wyvern Typesetting Ltd, Bristol

Printed in China

Introduction

Grammar Spectrum 2 is for pre-intermediate students of English. It explains and practises the grammar that pre-intermediate students need to learn. It can be used for self-study, for homework, and in class. This book is part of the *Grammar Spectrum* series of books; students can use the whole series to progress from an elementary to an intermediate level of English.

Using the book

When you have a particular grammar problem, you can look it up in the Contents at the front of the book, or in the Index at the back. You can then study the unit that deals with that problem. Or, you can work through the book from beginning to end.

Each unit begins with an explanation of the grammar point, and then it has a number of exercises for students to practise the grammar they have read about. Students can write their answers in the book, or on a separate piece of paper. When you have finished the exercises, you can check your answers in the answer key at the back of the book (page 102).

Form tables at the back of the book (pages 94–97) give information on Present Simple forms, -**ing** forms, past participles, etc.

Finishing the book

When you have finished studying the whole book, you can do the Exit tests on pages 98 to 101. In the Exit tests, every question tests something from a unit with the same number. If you make a mistake, for example in question 30, you can look back to unit 30 and study that unit again. The answers to the Exit tests are on page 117.

Enjoy your studies, and remember, when you have finished *Grammar Spectrum 2*, you are then ready to go on to *Grammar Spectrum 3*.

Contents

	Introduction		*page* 3
	Contents		4

Verbs and tenses

unit	**1**	Present Simple (**I start**)	6
	2	Present Continuous (**I'm working**)	8
	3	Present Simple (**I go**) or Present Continuous (**I'm going**)	10
	4	Past Simple (**I walked, she rang**)	12
	5	Past Continuous (**I was waiting**)	14
	6	Present Perfect (**I've finished**); **for, since**	16
	7	Present Perfect with **just, already, yet**	18
	8	Past Simple (**I lived**) or Present Perfect (**I have lived**)	20
	9	Present Perfect Continuous (**I've been cooking**)	22
	10	Past Perfect (**I had finished**)	24
	11	**Will** or **be going to**	26
	12	Present Continuous for the future (**I'm leaving tomorrow**)	28
	13	Conditionals (**If I am …**)	30
	14	Present tense verbs with **when, before, after, until** etc.	32
	15	**So am I. I am too. Neither am I. I'm not either.**	34
	16	Verb + preposition (**wait for, listen to**)	36
	17	**Make, do, have, get**	38

Sentences and questions

	18	Word order: subject, verb, object etc.	40
	19	**Who?** and **What?**: subject and object questions	42
	20	**How long? How far? How often? How much?** etc.	44
	21	Question tags (**It's cold, isn't it?**)	46

Modals and other verbs

	22	**Must, mustn't** (**I must leave**)	48
	23	**Have to** (**He has to go**)	50
	24	**Should, shouldn't** (**You shouldn't smoke**)	52
	25	**Can, could; may, might**	54

Passive

	26	Passive: Present Simple and Past Simple	56

Infinitives and -ing forms

unit **27** Verb + -**ing** (**I like cooking**); **like** and **would like**   *page* 58

28 To + infinitive (**I want to go**) or infinitive (**I can go**)   60

Reported speech

29 Reported speech; **say/said** or **tell/told**   62

Articles, nouns, pronouns etc.

30 Articles: **a/an, the**, or no article   64

31 **Myself, yourself** etc; **each other**   66

32 Direct and indirect objects (**She gave him a book**)   68

33 **Something, anybody, nothing** etc.   70

34 **All, most, some, none**   72

35 **Both** (**... and**), **either** (**... or**), **neither** (**... nor**)   74

Adjectives and adverbs

36 Comparative and superlative adjectives (**cheaper, the cheapest**)   76

37 Comparison: **as ... as** (**as strong as**)   78

38 **Too** and **enough** (**too big, big enough**)   80

39 Adjectives: -**ed** or -**ing** (**frightened** or **frightening**)   82

40 Adverbs (**slowly, fast**); comparative adverbs (**more quickly**)   84

41 Adverb + adjective (**very hot**); adjective + adjective; noun + noun
(**a cardboard box**)   86

Prepositions

42 Prepositions of place & movement (**in, to** etc.)   88

43 Prepositions: **in, with, by, without** (**by doing**)   90

Building sentences

44 Relative clauses with **who, which** or **that**   92

Form tables   94

Exit tests   98

Answer key to practice exercises   102

Answer key to exit tests   117

Index   118

Verb tenses table

1 Present Simple (**I start**)

1 We form the Present Simple in this way:

POSITIVE

I
You
We
They
} **start** at eight o'clock.

He
She
It
} **starts** at eight o'clock.

NEGATIVE

I
You
We
They
} **do not**
don't
} **start** at eight o'clock.

He
She
It
} **does not**
doesn't
} **start** at eight o'clock.

QUESTIONS

Do {
I
you
we
they
} **start** at 8?

Does {
he
she
it
} **start** at 8?

2 With **he/she/it** we add -**s** to most verbs:

walk → walks   get → gets   leave → leaves

But there are some exceptions:
► We add -**es** to verbs which end with -**sh**, -**ch**, -**ss** or -**o**:

finish → finishes   catch → catches
do → does   go → goes

► We change some verbs that end with -**y** in this way:

cry → cries   worry → worries
study → studies

► But we add -**s** to verbs that end with -**ay**, -**ey**, -**oy** or -**uy**:

pay → pays   play → plays   buy → buys

3 We use the Present Simple for facts:
*Secretaries **work** in offices.*
*Ruth **does** all her work very well.*
*It **doesn't snow** in this country.*

4 We use the Present Simple for repeated actions (e.g. habits, and events on a timetable):
*I usually **play** tennis at weekends.*
*Lessons **start** at 9 o'clock every morning.*

Practice

A Put the verbs in brackets ( ) into the correct forms of the Present Simple. For negative verbs, use the short forms (*don't, doesn't*). Sometimes you do not need to change the verb in brackets.

0 Tom __catches_____ (catch) the bus to school at about 9 o'clock.

1 It often _____ (rain) at this time of the year.

2 I _____ (not/drive) to work. I go by bus.

3 She usually _____ (have) lunch at about 1 o'clock.

4 He _____ (not/earn) much money in his job.

5 This problem _____ (not/happen) very often.

6 My father _____ (fly) to the USA regularly.

7 Trains to Oxford _____ (leave) every hour in the morning.

8 You _____ (not/do) your work carefully enough.

9 She _____ (read) a newspaper every day.

10 We _____ (not/listen) to the radio very often.

11 He often _____ (arrive) at work late.

12 They _____ (go) to a lot of concerts.

B **Complete the questions in the Present Simple.**

0 A: _Does Alan use_ a computer?

   B: Yes, Alan uses a computer.

1 A: _____ in an office?

   B: No, Carol works in a factory.

2 A: Where _____ your games?

   B: We play our games in the local park.

3 A: _____ the bus to school?

   B: Yes, I take the bus to school every morning.

4 A: When _____?

   B: The shops close at 5 o'clock in the afternoon.

5 A: _____ abroad on holiday every year?

   B: Yes, we go abroad every year.

6 A: _____ a lot of coffee every day?

   B: Yes, I drink about ten cups of coffee every day.

7 A: What kind of car _____?

   B: He drives an old German car.

8 A: When _____?

   B: The lessons finish at 4.30 every day.

C **Complete the dialogues using the Present Simple. For negative verbs, use short forms (*doesn't, don't*).**

0 A: Do you watch TV every evening?

   B: No, we _don't watch_ TV every evening.

1 A: Does Anna take the bus to work?

   B: Yes, she _____ the bus to work at 7 o'clock every morning.

2 A: What time do you have dinner in the evening?

   B: We usually _____ dinner at about 8 o'clock in the evening.

3 A: Do you often eat in restaurants?

   B: Yes, we often _____ in restaurants.

4 A: Where does Alison teach?

   B: She _____ at the university.

5 A: _____ here very often?

   B: No, I don't come here very often.

6 A: When _____ in the morning?

   B: The post arrives at 8 o'clock in the morning.

7 A: Do you play any sports?

   B: No, I _____ any sports. I don't like sport.

8 A: _____ to the office at weekends?

   B: No, she doesn't go to work at weekends.

9 A: Where _____ your car every evening?

   B: I park my car in the street outside my apartment.

2 Present Continuous (I'm working)

1 We form the Present Continuous in this way:

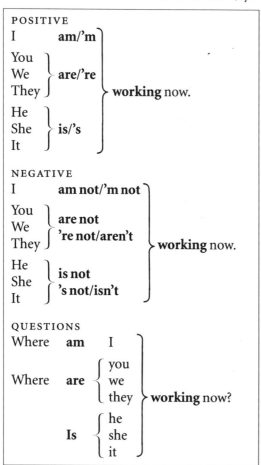

POSITIVE

I	am/'m	
You We They	are/'re	**working** now.
He She It	is/'s	

NEGATIVE

I	am not/'m not	
You We They	are not 're not/aren't	**working** now.
He She It	is not 's not/isn't	

QUESTIONS

Where	am	I	
Where	are	you we they	**working** now?
	Is	he she it	

2 To make the **-ing** form, we add **-ing**:

> walk → walking   go → going

There are some exceptions:
▶ verbs ending with **-e**:

> **-e → -ing: come → coming**

but: **see → seeing**
▶ verbs ending with **-ie**:

> **-ie → ying: lie → lying**

▶ verbs ending with one vowel (**a,e,i,o,u**) and one consonant (**b,c,d,f,g,k,l,m,n,p ...**):

> **-t → -tting: sit → sitting   run → running**

(For more details, see Table C, on page 95.)

3 Look at this picture of Mike:

We use the Present Continuous for things that are happening now:
> *Where's Mike? ~ He's sitting outside.*

We also use the Present Continuous for things that are happening for a period of time around now, but not at the moment we speak:
> *Mike is building his own house.*

....

Practice

A Complete the sentences about the pictures. Use the correct Present Continuous form of the verb in brackets, and *he/she/they*.

0 <u>He's drinking</u> (drink) a cup of coffee.
1 _____ (carry) their suitcases.
2 _____ (take) a photograph.
3 _____ (sit) on a bench.
4 _____ (run) in a race.
5 _____ (write) a letter.

B Complete the dialogues using the Present Continuous forms of the verbs in brackets ( ), and *I/you/he/she* etc.

0 A: What _are you watching_ (watch) on the TV?

   B: I'm watching a programme about wildlife in Africa.

1 A: What _____ (do) at the moment?

   B: He's reading a book.

2 A: _____ (listen) to me?

   B: Yes, of course I'm listening to you.

3 A: Where _____ (go)?

   B: I'm going to the shops.

4 A: What _____ (cook)?

   B: He's cooking an Italian dish.

5 A: Where _____ (stay)?

   B: She's staying with some friends.

6 A: _____ (wait) for the number 36 bus?

   B: No, I'm waiting for a different bus.

7 A: _____ (rain) at the moment?

   B: No, it's quite sunny now.

8 A: What _____ (read)?

   B: I'm reading a very interesting novel.

C Complete the dialogues using the Present Continuous forms of the words in brackets.

0 A: What's Jenny doing?

   B: _She's talking_ (She/talk) to her mother on the phone.

1 A: What are John and Michael doing?

   B: _____ (They/play) a game of cards.

2 A: _____ (the weather/get) better?

   B: No, it's very cold outside.

3 A: _____ (you/leave)?

   B: Yes, I have to go home now.

4 A: Where's Harry?

   B: _____ (He/make) a cup of coffee in the kitchen.

5 A: Where's your car?

   B: It's at home. _____ (It/not/work) at the moment.

6 A: _____ (you/watch) this programme?

   B: No, we can watch a different programme if you want.

7 A: Is Michael at home?

   B: No, _____ (he/post) some letters at the post office.

8 A: _____ (Paul/do) a course?

   B: Yes, he's studying Business Management.

3 Present simple (**I go**) or Present Continuous (**I'm going**)

Compare the Present Simple and the Present Continuous:

1

We use the Present Simple to talk about facts (things which are true at any time): *Anna **speaks** good Spanish.* *Journalists **write** newspaper articles.* *I **come** from Norway.* (= I am Norwegian).	We use the Present Continuous to talk about things that are happening now: *Anna's busy. She's **speaking** on the phone.* *What **are** you **writing?** ~ A letter to Jane.* *Look! The bus **is coming**.*

2

We use the Present Simple for situations that exist for a long time, and for actions that are repeated (e.g. people's habits, or events on a timetable): *Mike **works** for an advertising company. He **lives** in Paris.* (= His home is in Paris.)	We use the Present Continuous for things that continue for a limited period of time around now (e.g. holidays, visits, temporary jobs, school or university courses): *John **is working** in the USA for six weeks.* *He's **living** in New York.*

*Jane **travels** a lot in her job.* *I **do** a lot of sport.* We can use words like **usually, often, every:** *We **usually go** out to dinner at weekends.* *I **often go** to football matches on Sundays.* *The buses **leave every hour.***	*Jane's **travelling** around Europe for a month.* *I'm **doing** a one-year course in tourism.*

3

We use the Present Simple with thinking and feeling verbs (e.g. **know, like, want, love, hate, remember**): *I **don't know** which train to catch.*	We do not usually use the Present Continuous with thinking and feeling verbs: Not ~~I'm knowing someone who lives in Venice.~~

Practice

A **Complete the sentences with the Present Simple (*I do*) or the Present Continuous (*I am doing*).**

0 I __leave__ (leave) home at 7 o'clock every morning.

1 She usually _____ (work) in the Sales Department in London, but at the moment she _____ (do) a training course in Bristol.

2 Linda _____ (wash) her hair every day.

3 He _____ (try) very hard in every game that he _____ (play).

4 Excuse me. I think that you _____ (sit) in my seat.

5 _____ (you/listen) to the radio very often?

6 Don't talk to me now. I _____ (write) an important letter.

7 Why _____ (they/drive) on the left in Britain?

8 It _____ (not/get) dark at this time of year until about
   10 o'clock.

9 It usually _____ (rain) here a lot, but it
   _____ (not/rain) now.

10 A: What are you doing?
    B: I _____ (bake) a cake. Why _____ (you/smile)?
    _____ (I/do) something wrong?

B **Two people are standing on a railway station platform. Write the
   conversation between them, using the Present Simple or the Present
   Continuous. Sometimes, it is not necessary to change the verb form.**

Robert: (Hello. / you / wait / for the same train as me?)
         0 Hello. Are you waiting for the same train as me? _____

Paul: (I / not / know. I / wait / for the 6.15 to Brussels. And you?)
         1 _____

Robert: (Yes, me too. / you / live / in Brussels?)
         2 _____

Paul: (No. I come from Brussels, but I / study / at university in Paris at the moment.)
         3 _____

Robert: (Oh yes? What course / you / take?)
         4 _____

Paul: (I / do / a two-year course in Business Management.)
         5 _____

Robert: (So why / you / go / to Brussels?)
         6 _____

Paul: (All my friends / live / there, and I / often / go / there at weekends.)
         7 _____

         (I / not / know / many people in Paris. What about you? / you / often / go / to / Brussels?)
         8 _____

Robert: (Yes, on business. I / go / to a meeting there today.)
         9 _____

Paul: (Oh yes. What kind of job / you / do?)
         10 _____

Robert: (I / work / in the Marketing Department of a small company, and I / often / travel /
         to different towns and cities for meetings.)
         11 _____

Paul: (What / your company / sell?)
         12 _____

Robert: (It / make / clocks.)
         13 _____

Paul: (Oh look! The train / come.)
         14 _____

4 Past Simple (**I walked, she rang**)

1 We form the Past Simple of regular verbs by adding **-ed** to the verb:

walk → walked	watch → watched
open → opened	ask → asked

There are some exceptions:
- ▶ verbs ending with **-e**:

+ -d: live → lived	like → liked

- ▶ verbs ending with a consonant and **-y**:

-y → -ied: apply → applied	try → tried

- ▶ most verbs ending with one vowel and one consonant:

-p → -pped: stop → stopped	
	plan → planned

(For more details on the form of the Past Simple, see Table D on page 95.)

2 The Past Simple form of many verbs is irregular:

do → did	have → had
take → took	buy → bought
come → came	stand → stood
find → found	ring → rang
go → went	say → said

(For more details, see Table E, page 96.)

3 We form the negative with **didn't** and the infinitive (e.g. **do, take, understand**):
> I **didn't understand**. (Not ~~didn't understood~~)

We form questions with **did** and the infinitive (e.g. **watch**):
> **Did** you **watch** the film?

4 The Past Simple of **be** is like this:

I/he/she/it **was/wasn't**	⎱ very good.
You/we/they **were/weren't**	⎰
Was I/he/she/it	⎱ very good?
Were you/we/they	⎰

5 We use the Past Simple to talk about a completed event in the past. We often say when it happened (e.g. **yesterday, last night**):
> Chris **phoned** me **yesterday**. He **wanted** to discuss something with me.
> **Did** you **enjoy** the concert **last night**?

6 We can use the Past Simple with **for** to talk about something that continued for a period of time, and ended in the past:
> I **lived** in Rome **for two years**. Then I went to work in Japan.

past	1	2	3	4		now
		for 2 years				

Practice

A Complete the sentences using the Past Simple form and the words in brackets ( ).

0 We _went_ (go) on holiday to Scotland last year.

1 I _____ (take) a taxi from the airport to the city centre.

2 We _____ (walk) to the park and then we _____ (play) tennis.

3 A: _____ (be/your meal) good?

   B: No, it _____ (not-be). I _____ (not/like) the vegetables.

4 The man in the shop _____ (say) something to the woman, but she _____ (not/hear) him.

5 I _____ (ring) the doorbell and a woman _____ (open) the door.

6 I _____ (write) a letter to a friend, and then I _____ (post) it.

7 A: _____ (you/understand) the film?

   B: No. I _____ (try) to understand it, but the actors _____ (speak) very quickly.

8 He _____ (not/go) to school last Tuesday. He _____ (be) ill.

9 A: _____ (you/buy) some clothes at the market?

   B: Yes, I _____ (buy) a pair of trousers and a shirt.

10 A: _____ (you/enjoy) the festival?

    B: Yes. It _____ (not/rain) and the music _____ (be) very good.

B **Make sentences using the correct form of the Past Simple.**

  0 (When / you / leave / the party?)

    <u>When did you leave the party?</u>

  1 (When / you / finish / your exams?)

    _____

  2 (I / wait / for an hour, but he / not / phone.)

    _____

  3 (you / watch / the news on TV last night?)

    _____

  4 (Mark / stop / smoking last month, and he / start / playing tennis again last week.)

    _____

  5 (He / ask / me a question, but I / not / know / the answer.)

    _____

  6 (I / live / there for a few years, but I / not / like / the place.)

    _____

  7 (She / come / to my house yesterday, but she / not / stay.)

    _____

  8 (What / you / say? / I / not / hear / you.)

    _____

  9 (What / you / do / yesterday? / you / go / to school?)

    _____

C **It's the beginning of a new term at college. Two students, Nick and Eric, are talking about the summer holidays. Complete their conversation using the correct Past Simple form of the words in brackets ( ).**

Nick: What ⁰ <u>did you do</u> (you/do) in the summer?

Eric: I ¹_____ (take) a trip around Europe by train.

Nick: ²_____ (it/be) expensive?

Eric: No, I ³_____ (buy) a railcard, and it ⁴_____ (be) quite cheap.

Nick: ⁵_____ (you/go) on your own, or with some friends?

Eric: A couple of friends ⁶_____ (come) with me.

Nick: How many countries ⁷_____ (you/visit)?

Eric: I ⁸_____ (go) to six or seven countries. I ⁹_____ (have) a great time, and I really ¹⁰_____ (love) all of them.

Nick: Which one ¹¹_____ (you/like) most?

Eric: Sweden, I think. The countryside ¹²_____ (be) marvellous, and I ¹³_____ (take) lots of photographs.

Nick: When ¹⁴_____ (you/arrive) back home?

Eric: Last week. I'm still rather tired.

5 Past Continuous (**I was waiting**)

1 We form the Past Continuous in this way:

POSITIVE		
I/he/she/it	**was**	} **waiting.**
You/we/they	**were**	
NEGATIVE		
I/he/she/it	**was not/wasn't**	} **waiting.**
You/we/they	**were not/weren't**	
QUESTIONS		
Was	I/he/she/it	} **waiting?**
Were	you/we/they	

(For rules on the spelling of **-ing** forms (e.g. **waiting**), see Table C on page 95.)

2 Look at this example:

A: *What **were** you **doing** at 7 o'clock last night?*
B: *I **was driving** home from work.*

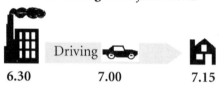

	Driving	
6.30	**7.00**	**7.15**

*I **was living** in Japan in 1991. (I lived there from 1990 to 1993.)*

We use the Past Continuous for an action or situation that was in progress at a particular time in the past (e.g. **at 7 p.m.**, **in 1991**).

3 Now look at this:

Ann   Keith

*When I **walked** into the room, Ann **was writing** postcards and Keith **was reading**.*

We use the Past Simple (**walked**) for a completed action. We use the Past Continuous (**was writing**) for an action in progress in the past.

4 We can use **when** or **while** before the Past Continuous:

*I met her **when/while** we **were working** for the same company.* (**when** = during the time)

We can only use **when** (not ~~while~~) before the Past Simple:

***When** I **met** her, we were working for the same company.* (**when** = at the time)

....

Practice

A Complete the sentences by putting the verbs in brackets ( ) into the Past Continuous.

0 It ___was snowing___ (snow) when I left home this morning.

1 I tried to explain my problem to her, but she _____ (not/listen).

2 He _____ (talk) on the phone when I arrived.

3 A lot of people _____ (wait) for the 7.30 bus last night.

4 I _____ (live) in London when I met them.

5 I nearly had an accident this morning. A car _____ (come) towards me, but I moved quickly out of the way.

6 At the end of the first half of the game, they _____ (win).

7 It was a sunny afternoon and people _____ (sit) on the grass in the park. Then it suddenly started to rain.

8 Which hotel _____ (you/stay) in when you lost your passport?

9 Fortunately, I _____ (not/drive) too fast when the child walked into the road in front of me.

10 I looked out of the window, and I saw that it _____ (not/rain)
    any more.

11 What _____ (you/do) at 3 o'clock yesterday afternoon?

B **Describe what the people in the picture were doing when Rick came into
   the room. Use the correct verb from the box in the Past Continuous.**

brush	watch	~~read~~
listen	write	eat
paint	sit	play

0 George __was reading__ a newspaper.   5 Barbara _____ a letter.

1 Julie _____ a sandwich.   6 Rita _____ her hair.

2 Sue and Liz _____ table tennis. 7 Alison _____ to some music.

3 Frank _____ television.   8 Ann _____ a picture.

4 Caroline _____ on the floor.

C **Look at this information about Shirley and Kevin and complete the sentences about
   them, using the Past Continuous (*I was doing*) or the Past Simple (*I did*).**

Shirley		Kevin	
1970–76	lived in New York	1972–80	lived in Washington
1973–76	studied at university	1973–75	did a course in Computing
1976	left university	1975–80	worked as a computer operator
1976–80	worked as a translator	1979	met Shirley
1979	met Kevin	1980–85	ran his own company
1982	married Kevin	1982	married Shirley

0 In 1972 Shirley __was living__ in New York.

1 In 1974 Kevin _____ in Washington.

2 In 1974 Shirley _____ at university.

3 In 1974 Kevin _____ a course in Computing.

4 When Shirley _____ university in 1976,
   Kevin _____ as a computer operator.

5 When Kevin _____ Shirley, she _____ as a translator.

6 While Shirley _____ as a translator, she _____ Kevin.

7 In 1982 Kevin _____ his own company.

8 While he _____ his own company, Kevin _____ Shirley.

6 Present Perfect (**I've finished**); for, since

1 We form the Present Perfect with **have** or **has** and a past participle (e.g. **finished**):

> POSITIVE
> I/you/we/they **have/'ve** ⎱ **finished.**
> He/she/it **has/'s** ⎰
>
> NEGATIVE
> I/you/we/they **haven't** ⎱ **finished.**
> He/she/it **hasn't** ⎰
>
> QUESTIONS
> **Have** I/you/we/they ⎱ **finished?**
> **Has** he/she/it ⎰

2 The past participle of regular verbs is the same as the Past Simple form:

> + -ed: wash → washed   start → started
> + -d: live → lived
> -y → -ied: reply → replied
>   study → studied
> -p → -pped: stop → stopped

(For more details, see Table D on page 95.)

For the past participles of irregular verbs, see Table E on page 96.

3 We use the Present Perfect to talk about something that happened in the past, but we do not say exactly when it happened:
> *I've seen this film before.* (**before** = before now)

We often use the Present Perfect in this way for things that happened in the past, and that have a result now:
> *I've seen this film before. I don't want to see it again now.*
> *She's left the company. She doesn't work there now.*

We often use the Present Perfect with **ever** (= at any time) and **never** (= at no time):
> *Have you **ever** met a famous person?*
> *He has **never** worked in a factory.*

4 We can use the Present Perfect with **for** and **since**, to talk about situations or actions in a period of time from the past until now. We use **for** with a period of time (e.g. **three months**), and **since** with a time (e.g. **Tuesday**):
> *We've lived here **for six months**.*

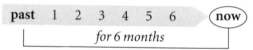

> *I haven't seen Tom **since Tuesday**.*

> | past | Mon. | (Tues.) | Wed. | | now |
> since Tuesday

Practice

A Look at the pictures that show what Jenny has done in her life. Complete the sentences about her, using the Present Perfect form of the verbs in brackets ( ).

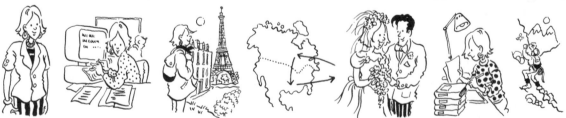

0 She ___has worked___ (work) as a secretary and as a schoolteacher.

1 She _____ (live) in Paris since 1991.

2 She _____ (visit) Canada and the USA.

3 She _____ (be) married for 4 years.

4 She _____ (write) four books.

5 She _____ (climb) Mont Blanc twice.

B   Complete the sentences using the Present Perfect form of the verbs in brackets ( ).

0   Don't take my plate away. I __haven't finished__ (not/finish) my meal.

1   A: What's that book about?

    B: I don't know. I _____ (not/read) it.

2   I _____ (lose) my pen. Can I borrow yours, please?

3   My father _____ (buy) an expensive, new car.

4   A: I _____ (book) a room here for tonight.

    B: Yes madam, what's your name, please?

5   I _____ (make) some sandwiches. Would you like one?

6   I'm not sure what the problem with the car is.

    It _____ (not/happen) before.

7   A: _____ (you/reply) to that letter from the bank?

    B: No I haven't, but I'll do it soon.

C   Write this conversation using the Present Perfect and the words in brackets ( ).

Rob: (you / ever / want / to work in another country?)

        0 _Have you ever wanted to work in another country?_

Brian: (Yes, in fact I / work / abroad.)

        1 _____

        (I / work / in Ireland and in Brazil.)

        2 _____

        (What about you? / you / ever / have / a job abroad?)

        3 _____

Rob: (No, I / never / want / to leave my home town.)

        4 _____

        (I / live / here for twenty years, and I / never / think / of working abroad.)

        5 _____

Brian: (Really? Well, I / apply / for another job abroad.)

        6 _____

D   Make sentences with the Present Perfect and *for* or *since*.

0   (I / not / play / tennis / last summer.)

    I haven't played tennis since last summer.

1   (I / know / her / more than ten years.)

    _____

2   (I / not / eat / anything / lunchtime.)

    _____

3   (you / live / in this town / a long time?)

    _____

4   (Jill / be / a good friend / we were at school together.)

    _____

5   (you / see / Jack / the party last week?)

    _____

7 Present Perfect with **just, already, yet**

1 We use **just** with the Present Perfect to talk about things that happened a short time before now:

have + **just** + PAST PARTICIPLE
It has **just** finished.

Could I speak to Jane, please? ~ I'm afraid she **has just left**.
(= She left a short time ago.)
Is that a good book? ~ I don't know. I**'ve just started** it.
(= I started it a short time before now.)

2 Look at this example with **already**:
Do you want something to eat? ~ No thanks, I**'ve already eaten**. (= I ate before now.)
We use **already** with the Present Perfect to emphasize that something happened before now, or before it was expected to happen. We use **already** like this:

have + **already** + PAST PARTICIPLE
I've **already** heard that story.

Here is another example:
Nicola: Is Sarah going to phone you later?
Robert: No. She's (= She has) already phoned me.
(= Sarah phoned before Nicola expected her to phone.)

3 We use **yet** with a negative verb to say that something has not happened, but we think that it will happen:

The post **hasn't arrived yet**. (= The post has not arrived, but it probably will arrive.)
I **haven't finished** this work **yet**. (= I haven't finished this work, but I will finish it.)
They **haven't replied** to my letter **yet**.

We use **yet** in questions to ask whether something, that we expect to happen, has happened:
Have you paid the bill **yet**? (= Perhaps you have not paid the bill, but you are going to pay it soon.)
Has it stopped raining **yet**? (= Perhaps it has not stopped raining, but it will stop raining soon.)
Have you found a job **yet**?

Notice that we usually put **yet** at the end of a negative statement or question:
They haven't replied to my letter **yet**.
Have you found a job **yet**?

....

Practice

A   Complete the dialogues, using *just* and the words in brackets ( ).
Use the Present Perfect.

0   A: What's happening in this programme?
   B: I don't know. <u>It's just started</u> (It/start).

1   A: _____ (I/come) back from my holiday.
   B: Did you have a good time?

2   A: Could I have a copy of *Sports World*, please?
   B: Sorry. _____ (I/sell) the last copy.

3   A: How's Lucy?
   B: She's very happy. _____ (She/finish) her exams.

4   A: _____ (I/have) a letter from Mike.
   B: Oh yes? What did he say?

5   A: Have you heard from Alison and Frank recently?
   B: Yes, _____ (they/move) to another town.

6 A: Have you still got the same car?

    B: No, _____ (I/buy) a new one.

7 A: Would you like something to eat?

    B: No, thanks. _____ (I/have) breakfast.

B **Make sentences using the Present Perfect with *already* or *yet*.**

  0 (I / not / read / today's newspaper.) yet

     <u>I haven't read today's newspaper yet.</u>

  1 (you / decide / which one to buy?) yet

     _____

  2 (I / explain / this to you three times.) already

     _____

  3 (Their baby son / start / talking.) already

     _____

  4 (you / phone / Jane?) yet

     _____

  5 (The game / not / finish) yet

     _____

  6 (I / have / lunch) already

     _____

  7 (He / spend / all his money) already

     _____

C **Complete the conversation using *just, already* or *yet* and the words in brackets ( ). Put the verbs into the Present Perfect.**

Julia: Are you having a good time here?

Anna: Yes, I haven't been here long, and ⁰ <u>I've already visited</u> _____ (I / visit) a lot of interesting places.

Julia: ¹_____ (you / visit / the Art Gallery /?)

Anna: No, ²_____ (I / not / do / that), but I'm going to do it.

Julia: What about the theatre? ³_____ (you / see / a play /?)

Anna: No, but ⁴_____ (I / book / a ticket) for one. It's called *The Friends*. I rang the theatre five minutes ago. Would you like to come with me?

Julia: Thanks, but ⁵_____ (I / see / that play). I saw it last month.

Anna: ⁶_____ (I / read) in the newspaper that *The Adventurers* are giving a concert next week. Do you think it will be good?

Julia: Yes. ⁷_____ (they / make) a really good, new record. It came out a couple of days ago.

Anna: Will I be able to get a ticket?

Julia: Yes. ⁸_____ (they / not / sell / all the tickets). But be quick! They're a very popular group.

8 Past Simple (**I lived**) or Present Perfect (**I have lived**)

Compare the Past Simple and the Present Perfect:

1

We use the Past Simple to talk about something that happened at a particular time in the past: *I **met** John **at 4 o'clock**.* *When **did** Jane **go** to India? ~ **In June**.* *Martin **bought** a new car **last week**.*	We use the Present Perfect to talk about the past, but not about when things happened: *I've **met** John's girlfriend. She's nice.* ***Have** you ever **been** to India? ~ Yes, I have.* *I **have** never **bought** a new car.*

2

We use the Past Simple for situations or actions during a period of time that ENDED in the past: *I **worked** there **for two years**. I left last year.*	We use the Present Perfect for situations or actions during a period of time from the past to NOW: *He **has worked** here **for two years**.* (He still works here.).

```
 past                           (now)
      |‾‾‾‾‾‾‾‾‾‾‾‾‾‾‾‾‾‾|
      | I worked there for 2 years. |
```

```
       past                     (now)
            |‾‾‾‾‾‾‾‾‾‾‾‾‾‾‾‾‾‾‾‾‾‾‾|
            | He has worked here for 2 years. |
```

*We **lived** in that house **for a long time**; then we moved to this one.*	*We've **lived** in this flat **since we got married**.* (We still live in it.)
*Our company **opened** two new shops **last summer**.*	*We opened two shops last summer.* ***Since then**, we **have opened** two more.* (**Since then** = since that time)

3 Notice how we often move from the Present Perfect to the Past Simple:

Peter: * **Have** you ever **played** this game before?*
Maria: *Yes, I **played** it once when I was in England.*
Peter: * **Did** you win?*
Maria: *No, I **lost**.*

....

Practice

A **Complete the conversation by choosing the correct form in brackets ( ).**

Sarah: <u>⁰ Have you ever been</u> (Have you ever been / Did you ever go) to the United States?

Jim: Yes, ¹_____ (I've been / I went) to California last year.

Sarah ²_____ (Have you liked / Did you like) it?

Jim: Yes, ³_____ (I've enjoyed / I enjoyed) the trip a lot.

Sarah: What ⁴_____ (have you done / did you do) there?

Jim: ⁵_____ (I've visited / I visited) Hollywood, Disneyland and San Francisco.

 ⁶_____ (Have you been / Did you go) to California, Sarah?

Sarah: No, but ⁷_____ (I've booked / I booked) a holiday there. I've got my ticket and I'm going next week!

B **Complete the dialogues using the Present Perfect (*I have seen*) or Past Simple (*I saw*).**

A: I ⁰ <u>saw</u> (see) Jack last night.

B: Oh really. I ¹_____ (not / see) him for months. How is he?

A: We ²_____ (go) to the theatre last Saturday.

B: ³_____ (you / enjoy) the play?

A: Yes, it ⁴_____ (be) very good.

A: I ⁵_____ (never / hear) of this group before. Are they famous in your country?

B: Yes, they are very popular. They ⁶_____ (be) famous in my country for years.

A: What ⁷_____ (you / do) last weekend?

B: I ⁸_____ (stay) at home. I ⁹_____ (need) a rest.

A: ¹⁰_____ (you / ever / win) a competition?

B: Yes, I ¹¹_____ (win) a photographic competition in 1992.

A: So, John is your best friend. ¹²_____ (you / meet) him when you were at university?

B: Yes. We ¹³_____ (be) friends for more than ten years.

C **Complete this paragraph about the London Underground by putting in the Present Perfect or Past Simple forms of the verbs in brackets ( ).**

The London Underground

London ⁰ <u>has had</u> (have) an underground train system since the 19th Century. The London Underground ¹_____ (start) in 1863, when Victorian engineers and workers ²_____ (build) the Metropolitan railway. This railway line ³_____ (go) from Paddington Station to Farringdon Street Station, and steam engines ⁴_____ (pull) the coaches. Eight more lines ⁵_____ (open) since then. The world's first underground electric railway ⁶_____ (open) in 1890. This line ⁷_____ (go) from the City of London to Stockwell in South London. The most modern line is the Jubilee line, which ⁸_____ (open) in 1977. Since the London Underground ⁹_____ (begin), many other cities, such as New York and Moscow, ¹⁰_____ (build) their own systems.

9 Present Perfect Continuous (**I've been cooking**)

1 We form the Present Perfect Continuous in this way:

> POSITIVE
> I/you/we/they **have/'ve** } been cooking.
> He/she/it **has/'s**
>
> NEGATIVE
> I/you/we/they **haven't** } been cooking.
> He/she/it **hasn't**
>
> QUESTIONS
> **Have** I/you/we/they } been cooking?
> **Has** he/she/it

(For details about **-ing** forms see Table C, on page 95.)

2 We use the Present Perfect Continuous for an action or situation that began in the past and continues until now:

> *You're late! I've been waiting for you.*

We often use **for** and **since** with the Present Perfect Continuous. We use **for** with a period of time, and **since** with a point in time:

> *I've been waiting for you **for two hours**.*
> *I've been waiting for you **since 6 o'clock**.*

3 Here are some more examples:

PAST   NOW

> *Julia **has been talking** on the phone for an hour.* (= She started talking on the phone an hour ago and she is still talking.)

> *You**'ve been sitting** there since 1 o'clock.* (= You started sitting there at one o'clock and you are still sitting there.)

4 We use the Present Perfect Continuous for actions that are done many times in a period of time from the past until now:

> *She**'s been having** driving lessons for a couple of months.* (= She started a couple of months ago; she is still having lessons.)
> *I**'ve been playing** tennis since I was a small child.*

5 We can use **How long** with the Present Perfect Continuous:

> *How long **have** you **been living** here?*

••

Practice

A Write a sentence for each of the following situations, using the Present Perfect Continuous and *for* or *since*.

0 She started her course a month ago and she is still doing it.

  She has been doing her course for a month.

0 I started reading this novel last weekend and I'm still reading it.

  I have been reading this novel since last weekend.

1 It started raining at 3 o'clock and it is still raining.

  _____

2 He started playing chess when he was 10 and he still plays it.

  _____

3 I started work at 8 o'clock and I'm still working.

  _____

4 Helen started looking for another job two months ago and she's still looking.

  _____

5 We arrived here two hours ago and we're still waiting.

  _____

B Put *for* or *since* into the gaps.

0 I've been working in this office <u>since</u> last summer.

1 Have you been doing this course _____ a long time?

2 I've been driving this car _____ more than ten years.

3 She has been planning the party _____ the beginning of the month.

4 George has been telling the same stories _____ several years.

5 We've been waiting for a reply _____ we wrote to them last week.

6 What have you been doing _____ the last time that I saw you?

7 You've been writing that letter _____ more than two hours.

8 He's been feeling ill _____ a few days.

C Complete these dialogues by putting the verbs in brackets ( ) into the Present Perfect Continuous.

A: When did you arrive in London?

B: Two weeks ago.

A: Where ⁰ <u>have you been staying</u>_____ (you/stay)?

B: I ¹_____ (stay) with some friends in their flat.
   But I am going to move to my own flat next week.

A: Hallo. What are you doing here?

B: I'm waiting to see the manager. I ²_____
   (wait) for half an hour.

A: She's very busy. She ³_____ (talk) on the
   phone to someone all afternoon.

A: I didn't know that you could play the piano.

B: Oh yes, I ⁴_____ (have) piano lessons for a year.

A: How long ⁵_____ (you/look) for a job?

B: I started looking immediately after I lost my old job. I
   ⁶_____ (apply) for jobs for about six months.

D Choose the best verb from the box to complete each sentence. Use the Present Perfect Continuous form of the verb.

rain	save	study	read
make	~~learn~~	watch	play

0 She <u>has been learning</u> Spanish for six months.

1 It _____ for hours; the roads are very wet.

2 We _____ this game for hours. Let's stop!

3 Wendy _____ French at school for three years.

4 I _____ this book for months, but I haven't finished it yet.

5 We _____ this programme for hours.

6 The people next door _____ a lot of noise all day.

7 I _____ my money for a holiday.

10 Past Perfect (**I had finished**)

1 We form the Past Perfect with **had** and a past participle (e.g. **finished**, **gone**):

POSITIVE		
I/you/he/she/it/we/they	**had**	gone.

NEGATIVE		
I/you/he/she/it/we/they	**hadn't**	gone.

QUESTIONS		
Had	I/you/he/she/it/we/they	gone?

(For details on past participle forms, see Table D on page 95, and Table E on page 96.)

2 Look at this example:
*Jane **had gone** home when I phoned her at the office.* (= First, Jane went home. Later, I phoned her.)

past   now

Jane went home.   *I phoned her.*

3 We use the Past Perfect (e.g. **had gone**) for something that happened before something else in the past. We use the Past Perfect for the thing that happened first; we use the Past Simple (e.g. **phoned**) for the thing that happened later.

Here are some more examples:
*When I got home, I saw that the letter **had arrived**.* (= First, the letter arrived. Later, I got home and I saw it.)

*When he **had finished** his homework, he went to bed.* (= First, he finished his homework. Later, he went to bed.)

*He couldn't pay the bill because he **had left** his wallet at home.* (= First, he left his wallet at home. Later, he couldn't pay the bill.)

*I was very nervous because I **hadn't driven** a car on the motorway **before**.* (**before** = before then)

Note also this example with **by the time** (= when): ***By the time** he was twenty-five, he **had made** a million pounds.*

....

Practice

A Complete the sentences using the Past Perfect forms of the verbs in brackets ( ).

0 I didn't watch the film because I <u>had seen</u> (see) it before.

1 We couldn't eat at the restaurant because we _____ (not/book) a table.

2 I couldn't buy it because I _____ (spend) all my money.

3 I was tired because I _____ (get up) very early that morning.

4 He didn't know the answer because he _____ (not / do) his homework.

5 She was very happy because she _____ (win) a prize.

6 I _____ (forget) my pen so I had to borrow one.

7 When I got home, I switched on the answerphone. Several people _____ (leave) messages for me.

8 I _____ (not/hear) the joke before; I laughed a lot.

9 When we came out of the restaurant, we saw that our car _____ (disappear).

10 She couldn't see the photographs very well because she _____ (not/bring) her glasses.

11 The ground was very dry; it _____ (not/rain) for a long time.

B Henry invited some friends to his flat for a meal. Look at the things that he did and didn't do, before his guests arrived. Complete the phrases, using the Past Perfect.

0	He bought the food.
1	He cleaned the flat.
2	He didn't buy anything to drink.
3	He had a shower.
4	He changed his clothes.
5	He started preparing the meal.
6	He didn't finish preparing the meal.

By the time his guests arrived:

0   he had bought the food.

1   _____

2   _____

3   _____

4   _____

5   _____

6   _____

C Complete the sentences so that they mean the same as the pairs of sentences above them. Use the Past Perfect and the Past Simple.

0   We finished our meal. Then we went for a walk.

When we had finished our meal, we went for a walk. _____

1   I did the course. Then I was able to speak the language well.

When I _____

2   He did all his work. Then he went home.

When _____

3   Everyone left. Then I went to bed.

When _____

4   She had a glass of water. Then she felt better.

When _____

5   He did the washing-up. Then he listened to some music.

When _____

6   Steve saved enough money. Then he bought a new motorbike.

When _____

7   I discussed the problem with a friend. Then I felt happier.

I felt happier when _____

8   She finished speaking. Then I gave my opinion.

I _____ when she _____

9   The guests left. Then we tidied the house.

We _____ when _____

11 Will or be going to

Compare **will** and **be going to**:

1

We use **will** with an infinitive (**do, go, be, arrive** etc.):	We use **be going** with **to** + infinitive (**to do, to be, to rain** etc.):
 John **will** [INFINITIVE **arrive**] tomorrow.	It's going [to + INFINITIVE **to rain**] soon.
I/you/he (etc.) **will/'ll go.**	*My friends **are going to come** tonight.*
I/you/he (etc.) **will not/won't go.**	*It **isn't going to rain** today.*
Will I/you/he (etc.) **go?**	*What **are** you **going to do** on Sunday?*

2

We use **will** for actions that we decide to do NOW, at the moment of speaking:	We use **be going to** for actions that we have decided to do BEFORE we speak:
past → now speaking/decision	past → now decision / speaking
*I like this coat. I think **I'll buy** it.*	*I'm going to clean my room this afternoon.*
A: *What would you like to eat?*	(I decided to clean it this morning.)
B: ***I'll have** a pizza, please.*	
We can use **will** for offers and promises:	We can ask questions about people's plans:
***I'll carry** your case for you.* (offer)	*Which train **are you going to catch**?*
***I won't forget** your birthday again.* (promise)	(= Which train have you decided to catch?)

3

We use **will** to talk about things that we think or believe will happen in the future:	We use **be going to** for something that we expect to happen, because the situation now indicates that it is going to happen:
I'm sure you'll enjoy the film.	*He's running towards the goal, and he's going*
*I'm sure it **won't rain** tomorrow. It'll be another beautiful, sunny day.*	***to score.***

....

Practice

A Look at the pictures and complete the sentences about what we can see is
going to happen. Use *be going to* and the words in the box.

take	catch
~~eat~~	land
jump	knock

0   He's going to eat _____ his meal.

1   The plane _____ .

2   She _____ a picture.

3   He _____ into the water.

4   She _____ on the door.

5   He _____ the ball.

B **Make sentences with 'll and the words in brackets ( ).**

0 Sit down. (I / make / you a cup of coffee.) _I'll make you a cup of coffee._

1 A: It's time for me to go home.

   B: (I / give / you a lift.) _____

2 (I / phone / you tonight, I promise.) _____

3 A: I won't be able to buy the tickets for the concert today.

   B: Don't worry. (I / buy / the tickets for both of us, and I / meet / you at the concert hall.) _____

4 A: Oh no, it's raining and I must go to the shops.

   B: That's okay. (I / lend / you my umbrella.) _____

C **Complete these sentences using the correct form of *am/is/are going to* and the words in brackets ( ).**

0 I keep sneezing. I _'m going to get_ _____ (get) a bad cold.

1 Some of my friends _____ (have) a party next week. They've invited lots of people.

2 I _____ (play) tennis this afternoon. I've booked a court.

3 We _____ (move) to a different area of the town because we don't like this area.

4 Anna _____ (look) for a different job. She wants to do something more interesting.

5 They said on the radio that it _____ (rain) this afternoon.

D **Complete the sentences, using the words in brackets and 'll or a form of *be going to*.**

0 A: It's rather hot in here, isn't it?

   B: Yes, you're right. _I'll open_ _____ (I/open) a window.

1 A: Are you going to watch TV tonight?

   B: Yes, _____ (I/watch) my favourite programme at 9 o'clock.

2 A: What _____ (you/eat) tonight? What food have you bought?

   B: I haven't bought any food.

   A: Well, why don't you come to my house? _____ (I/cook) us something nice to eat.

3 A: I'm going into the centre of town tomorrow. _____ (I/buy) some new clothes.

   B: Oh, what _____ (you/get)?

   A: _____ (I/look) for a T-shirt and some jeans.

   B: I'd like to go into the centre too. _____ (I/come) with you.

4 A: _____ (I/leave) work late tomorrow. There is a meeting at 6 p.m.

   B: Oh, I didn't know that. Well, _____ (I/see) you after the meeting.

5 _____ (I/phone) Tom at 6 o'clock. I promised to phone him this evening.

6 A: Are you going to have a holiday in the summer?

   B: Yes, _____ (I/travel) around Europe with a friend.

12 Present Continuous for the future (I'm leaving tomorrow)

1 We can use the Present Continuous (see unit 2) to talk about the future:
  A: *Where **are** you **going** next week?*
  B: *We're **flying** to Switzerland. We're **staying** in the Alps for a week.*

2 We use the Present Continuous to talk about future arrangements. Arrangements are plans of action that we have agreed with other people:
  *I'm **meeting** some friends at a disco tonight.*
  (= I have talked to my friends, and we have agreed a time and place to meet.)

  *Mary **is starting** a course on Monday.*
  (= She has registered at a school for a particular course.)

  *He's **getting** a new car on Monday.*
  (= He has chosen the car and has arranged to buy it.)

  *I'm **not doing** anything this weekend.*
  (= I have no particular plans; I haven't arranged to do anything.)

3 When we talk about future plans, we can often use either the Present Continuous or **be going to**, but compare:

PRESENT CONTINUOUS:
*We're **moving** to a new flat in two weeks.* (= We have found the flat, signed the contract, and agreed a date to move.)
be going to: *We're **going to move** to a new flat soon.* (= We intend to move but we don't know when; we have not found a flat.)

  We use the Present Continuous for a definite arrangement. We use **be going to** for something that we intend to do, but that we may not have arranged. Here is another example:

*I'm **meeting** Diana at 3 p.m., and I'm **going to meet** her assistant some time next week. (= I have arranged to meet Diana, and I intend to meet her assistant.)*

Practice

A **These are the arrangements for a trip that you and a friend are taking next week.**

4-Day trip to Madrid	
Tuesday:	flight leaves at 18.00; check in at the *Hotel Princess*
Wednesday:	visit the Prado Museum, morning; take a guided tour of the Royal Palace, afternoon
Thursday:	have a special lunch at the hotel; see an opera at the Opera House, evening
Friday:	leave Madrid at 11.00.

Complete these sentences using the Present Continuous form of these verbs:

have   ~~go~~   see   fly   stay   leave   take   visit

0 ___We're going___ on a 4-day trip to Madrid next week.
1 _____ to Madrid at 18.00 on Tuesday.
2 _____ in the Hotel Princess.
3 _____ the Prado Museum on Wednesday morning.
4 _____ a guided tour of the Royal Palace on Wednesday afternoon.
5 _____ a special lunch at the hotel on Thursday.
6 _____ an opera at the Opera House on Thursday evening.
7 _____ Madrid at 11.00 on Friday.

B   Look at this page from Laura's diary for next week and complete the
    sentences about her plans, using the Present Continuous.

Monday:	work until 6 o'clock; go to the library after work.
Tuesday:	play tennis with Ian, 5 o'clock.
Wednesday:	go to the doctor's, 2.30
Thursday:	have a typing lesson, 10.30–12.30
Friday:	meet Jackie outside cinema, 8.30. Film starts at 9.
Saturday:	Nick & Lucy come here for dinner
Sunday:	_____

0   _She's working_____ until 6 on Monday.

1   _____ to the library after work on Monday.

2   _____ tennis with Ian at 5 on Tuesday.

3   _____ to the doctor's at 2.30 on Wednesday.

4   _____ a typing lesson from 10.30 to 12.30 on Thursday.

5   _____ Jackie outside the cinema at 8.30 on Friday.

6   _____ a film at 9 on Friday.

7   Nick and Lucy _____ to her house for dinner on Saturday.

8   _____ anything on Sunday.

C   Look at George's timetable for tomorrow and complete the conversation
    that follows it, using the Present Continuous and the words in brackets ( ).

9 o'clock:	catch the train
10 o'clock:	meet Judy in the main square
11 o'clock:	meet Harry and Fred for coffee
12 o'clock:	go to the theatre box office for tickets
1 o'clock:	have lunch with Dave
2–5 o'clock:	help Dave in his bike shop
6 o'clock:	catch the train home

Tim: What ⁰ _are you doing_____ (you/do) tomorrow, George?

George: ¹_____ (I/go) into the town centre.

Tim: What time ²_____ (you/catch) the train?

George: At 9 o'clock. ³_____ (I/meet) Judy at 10.

Tim: Where ⁴_____ (you/meet) her?

George: In the main square, and then ⁵_____ (we/meet) Harry and

          Fred in a café. After that, ⁶_____ (we/go) to the theatre to buy

          some tickets, and then ⁷_____ (I/have) lunch with Dave.

Tim: What ⁸_____ (you/do) in the afternoon?

George: ⁹_____ (I/help) Dave in his shop.

Tim: When ¹⁰_____ (you/come) home?

George: ¹¹_____ (I/catch) the train back at 6.

13 Conditionals (**If I am . . .**)

1 Look at this:

If + PRESENT SIMPLE + PRESENT SIMPLE
If   *I **eat** too much,*   *I **feel** bad.*

(= Every time I eat too much, I feel bad.)

We use this structure (**if** + Present Simple, + Present Simple) for facts that are generally true:
*If I **don't get** enough sleep, I **feel** tired.*
(= Every time I don't get enough sleep, I feel tired.)
*If you **want** to become a doctor, you **have** to study hard.* (= Anyone who wants to become a doctor has to study hard.)

2 We can say the same thing by reversing the two parts of the sentence:

PRESENT SIMPLE + if + PRESENT SIMPLE
*I **feel** bad*   *if*   *I **eat** too much.*

Note that we do not use a comma (,) before **if**.

3 Now look at this:

If + PRESENT SIMPLE + **will/won't**
If   *I'**m** late,*   *she'**ll be** angry.*

(= Perhaps I will be late; then she'll be angry.)

We use this structure (**if** + Present Simple + **will/won't**) to talk about things that may happen in the future. The verb after **if** is Present Simple, but we use it for a possible future action or situation; we use **will/won't** + verb for the result:

future possibility + result
If   *we **don't hurry**,*   *we **won't finish**.*

4 We can reverse the order:
*She'll be angry **if** I'm late.*
*We won't finish **if** we don't hurry.*

5 We do not use **will/won't** after **if**:
Not ~~If I will be late, she'll be angry.~~

....

Practice

A Put these facts about various types of people into sentences with **if** + Present Simple, + Present Simple. Make **you** the subject of both parts of the sentence.

0 Doctors treat people who are ill.

   <u>If you're a doctor, you treat people who are ill.</u>

1 Vegetarians don't eat meat.

   If you're a vegetarian, _____

2 People who live in a hot country don't like cold weather.

   If you live _____

3 Teachers have to work very hard.

   If you're a teacher, _____

4 People who do a lot of exercise stay fit and healthy.

   If you _____

5 Mechanics understand engines.

   If you're a _____

6 People who read newspapers know what's happening in the world.

_____

B Complete these sentences with *if* + Present Simple, + *will/won't,* using the words in brackets. Sometimes you do not need to change the words in brackets ( ).

0 If _it rains_____ (it/rain), _we won't go_____ (we/not/go) out.

1 If _____ (the weather/be) nice tomorrow, _____ (we/drive) to the coast.

2 If _____ (she/post) the letter now, _____ (they/receive) it tomorrow.

3 _____ (the boss/be) angry if _____ (John/arrive) at work late again.

4 _____ (I/go) to their party if _____ (I/have) enough time.

5 If _____ (she/not/pass) this exam, _____ (she/not/get) the job that she wants.

6 _____ (you/learn) a lot if _____ (you/take) this course.

7 If _____ (I/get) a ticket, _____ (I/go) to the concert.

8 _____ (I/buy) that camera if _____ (it/not/cost) too much.

9 If _____ (you/run) very fast, _____ (you/catch) the bus.

10 _____ (I/go) to the doctor's if _____ (I/not/feel) better tomorrow.

11 If _____ (they/win) this game, _____ (they/be) the champions.

C Complete the dialogues with the Present Simple or *will/won't* forms of the words in brackets ( ). Sometimes you do not need to change the words in brackets.

0 A: We must be at the airport at 2 o'clock.
   B: Well, if _we take_____ (we/take) a taxi at 1 o'clock,
      _we won't be_____ (we/not/be) late.

1 A: I'd like a newspaper.
   B: Well, _____ (I/buy) one for you if
      _____ (I/go) to the shop later.

2 A: Has John phoned yet?
   B: No, and if _____ (he/not/phone) this
      afternoon, _____ (I/phone) him this evening.

3 A: Is Fiona there, please?
   B: No, but if _____ (you/want) to leave a message,
      _____ (I/give) it to her.

4 A: Is Tim going to pass his exam?
   B: Well, _____ (he/fail) if
      _____ (he/not/work) harder.

5 A: Could I have some information about this year's concerts, please?
   B: Yes, if _____ (you/fill in) this form,
      _____ (I/send) it to you in the post.

14 Present tense verbs with **when**, **before**, **after**, **until** etc.

1 Look at this sentence:

When the programme **ends**, I'll do the washing-up.

To talk about an event in the future, we usually use the Present Simple (e.g. **ends**) after **when**, **before**, **after**, **until** and **as soon as**. We do not use **will**:

I'm going to finish this work **before** I **go**. (Not *... before I will go.*)
Wait here **until** I **get** back.
I'll phone you **as soon as** I **arrive**.

2 We can use **when** + Present Simple to refer to a time when something will happen:

I'll buy an ice-cream **when** I'm in the newsagent's.

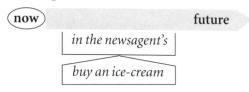

When you **see** her, give her my message.

We use **until** + Present Simple to mean from now to a time in the future:

We'll sit outside **until** it **gets** dark. (= We'll sit outside from now to when it gets dark.)

We use **as soon as** + Present Simple with the meaning 'immediately after':

They'll start playing **as soon as** it **stops** raining. (= They will start playing immediately after the rain stops.)

3 We use **when** + Present Perfect (e.g. I **have done**) to talk about an action that must, or will, happen before the next action can happen:

When I've **found** a job, I'll look for a place to live. (= First I will find a job; then I will look for a place to live.)

When Simon **has saved** enough money, he'll buy a car. (= First Simon must save the money; then he can buy a car.)

4 With **after** we can use either the Present Simple or the Present Perfect with no difference in meaning:

After she **takes/has taken** the course, she'll be a qualified teacher. (= When she has done her course, she'll be a qualified teacher.)

Practice

A Complete the sentences by putting *when, before, after, as soon as* or *until* into the gaps. Sometimes more than one answer is possible.

0 I'll stay in this job __until__ I find a better one.

1 I'm going to keep working _____ I finish this.

2 Remember to buy some stamps _____ you're in the post office.

3 _____ I speak to him on the phone tonight, I'll ask him.

4 We can go for a meal _____ we've seen the film.

5 I'll keep looking for it _____ I find it.

6 I'll wait for them _____ it gets dark, and then I'll leave.

7 Don't forget to lock the door _____ you go out.

8 _____ I've found the information, I'll phone you.

9 We'll wait _____ it stops raining, and then we'll go out.

10 _____ you see John, give him my regards.

11 Put in your application _____ the closing date arrives.

12 You shouldn't wait. You should reply _____ you receive the invitation.

13 Book a table _____ you go to the restaurant. It's often full.

B Complete the dialogues, using the Present Simple or *will* forms of the
   verbs in brackets ( ). Sometimes you do not need to change the word in
   brackets.

0 A: Could you post this letter for me today, please?
   B: Yes, I _'ll do_____ (do) it when I _go_____ (go) to the shops.

1 A: I might be late tonight.
   B: OK. I _____ (wait) until you _____ (arrive).

2 A: I'm leaving next week.
   B: I _____ (see) you before you _____ (go), won't I?

3 A: Have you decided what you're going to do at the weekend yet?
   B: No, but I _____ (phone) you as soon as I _____ (know)
      what I'm going to do.

4 A: Have you done that homework yet?
   B: No, not yet. I _____ (do) it when I _____ (have) enough time.

5 A: I don't want to go to that party tonight.
   B: Well, I'm sure you _____ (enjoy) it when you
      _____ (get) there.

6 A: Could you tell Tom to ring me, please?
   B: Yes, I _____ (tell) him when I _____ (see) him tomorrow.

7 A: Mr Jackson isn't in at the moment.
   B: I see. Well, I _____ (wait) until he _____ (come) back.

8 A: Have you booked a hotel in London yet?
   B: No, but we _____ (book) one before we _____ (go) there.

9 A: Don't forget to write to Peter.
   B: OK. I _____ (do) it as soon as I _____ (get) home.

10 A: _____ (you/see) Jack when you _____ (be) in Madrid?
   B: Yes, I hope I will. I _____ (phone) him when I _____ (arrive) in
      Madrid.

C Complete the sentences using the Present Perfect or *will* forms of the verbs
   in brackets.

0 When you _have written_____ (write) that letter, I'll _post_____ (post) it for you.

1 I _____ (pay) the bill when I have borrowed some money from somebody.

2 When I've found a car that I want to buy, I _____ (ask) my bank to lend me
   the money to buy it.

3 After the plane _____ (land), you may unfasten your safety belts.

4 When you _____ (check) all your answers, hand in your question paper.

5 I _____ (read) this book when I'm on holiday.

6 When I _____ (read) this magazine, I'll start work.

7 You _____ (feel) better when you have had something to eat.

8 When you _____ (finish) your work, you can go home.

9 She _____ (be) pleased when she hears the news.

10 Let's go for a walk after we _____ (have) dinner.

15 So am I. I am too. Neither am I. I'm not either.

1 Look at this:

(I'm tired.) (So am I.)

She is saying that she is also tired.

2 Here are some more examples:

He **was** very angry. ~ *So **was** I.*

My flat's quite small. ~ *So **is** mine.*
They **were** waiting. ~ *So **was** she.*
I'm going to have tea. ~ *So **am** I.*

Ann **has** finished her work and so **has Mary**.
They've **been** waiting ~ *So **has** she.*

I **work** in an office ~ *So **do** I.*
I **enjoyed** the film. ~ *So **did** I.*

Philip **will** pass the exam and so **will you**.
He **can** drive. ~ *So **can** she.*

Note:
▶ we use **so** after a positive statement;
▶ the verb we use after **so** depends on the verb used in the positive statement.

3 Instead of **so am I**, we can say **I am too**, with the same meaning. Here are some examples:

I'm tired. ~ *I **am** too.*
We've got a small flat. ~ *We **have** too.*
I work in an office. ~ *I **do** too.*
Bill enjoyed the film and **I did** too.
He can drive. ~ *She **can** too.*

4 We can use expressions like **neither am** I to reply to a negative statement:

I'm not tired. ~ *Neither **am** I.*
(= And I'm not tired.)
I haven't seen that film ~ *Neither **have** I.*
I don't like this place. ~ *Neither **do** I.*
I didn't see that play. ~ *Neither **did** I.*
His sister can't drive and neither **can he**.

5 We can say **I'm not either** to mean the same as **neither am** I:

I'm not tired. ~ *I'm not either.*
(= And I'm not tired.)
I haven't seen that film. ~ *I **haven't** either.*
I don't like this place. ~ *I **don't** either.*
I didn't see that play. ~ *I **didn't** either.*
His sister can't drive and **he can't** either.

Practice

A **Complete the sentences with *so, too, either* or *neither*.**

0 I really enjoyed that meal. ~ _So_____ did I.

0 I haven't done the homework. ~ I haven't _either_____.

0 We live in the centre of town. ~ We do _too_____.

1 I don't like football. ~ _____ do I.

2 I haven't been to America. ~ _____ have I.

3 My father works in an office. ~ _____ does mine.

4 I haven't read a newspaper today. ~ _____ have I.

5 I play a lot of different sports. ~ I do _____.

6 I've been working very hard lately. ~ _____ have I.

7 Ann will be at the party and _____ will Jane.

8 My brother can't speak any foreign languages and _____ can my sister.

9 Helen sent me a birthday card and Robin did _____.

10 George isn't going to the meeting and I'm not _____.

11 Tony arrived late and _____ did I.

12 Kathy didn't go to the concert and _____ did I.

B Put in the replies, using *so* or *neither* and the words in brackets, as in the examples.

	QUESTIONS			ANSWERS
0	I've got a cold.	(I)	~	So have I.
0	I haven't got much money.	(I)	~	Neither have I.
1	We're going to the concert.	(we)	~	_____
2	My pen doesn't work.	(mine)	~	_____
3	I haven't read today's paper.	(I)	~	_____
4	My meal was excellent.	(mine)	~	_____
5	I've been ill.	(Frank)	~	_____
6	Ron didn't go to the party.	(George)	~	_____
7	I can't understand this game.	(I)	~	_____
8	I'm not working tomorrow.	(I)	~	_____
9	Ruth passed the exam.	(John)	~	_____
10	I've eaten enough.	(I)	~	_____
11	I'm going to see that film.	(we)	~	_____
12	My car is very old.	(mine)	~	_____

C Look at the information in the table about four people and complete the sentences using *so, too, either* or *neither*.

	JULIA	ROBERT	SANDRA	PAUL
Lives in:	New York	Chicago	New York	Los Angeles
Speaks:	Spanish	French	Spanish	French
Drives?	Yes	No	No	Yes
Likes:	reading	travelling	travelling	reading
Plays:	basketball	basketball	tennis	tennis

0 Julia lives in New York and Sandra _does too_____ .

0 Julia lives in New York and _so does_____ Sandra.

1 Robert doesn't live in New York and _____ Paul.

2 Robert doesn't live in New York and Paul _____ .

3 Julia speaks Spanish and _____ Sandra.

4 Julia speaks Spanish and Sandra _____ .

5 Robert can't speak Spanish and _____ Paul.

6 Robert can't speak Spanish and Paul _____ .

7 Julia can drive and Paul _____ .

8 Robert can't drive and _____ Sandra.

9 Julia has passed her driving test and _____ Paul.

10 Robert likes travelling and _____ Sandra.

11 Julia likes reading and Paul _____ .

12 Julia plays basketball and _____ Robert.

13 Sandra doesn't play basketball and _____ Paul.

16 Verb + preposition (**wait for, listen to**)

1 After some verbs we use a particular preposition (e.g. **for, to, on**):

> VERB + PREPOSITION
> **wait for**: *I was **waiting for** a bus.*
> **listen to**: *She **listens to** the radio a lot.*
> **belong to**: *Does that book **belong to** you?*
> **ask for**: *Have you **asked for** the bill?*
> **apply for**: *He has **applied for** another job.*
> **depend on**: *The salary **depends on** your age.*
> **agree with**: *I don't **agree with** you.*

2 Now look at these examples:
> ▶ **arrive at / in:**
> *We **arrived at** the **airport**.* (You **arrive at** a place, for example a building.)
> *We **arrived in** Portugal.* (You **arrive in** a town or country.)
> ▶ **look at / for:**
> ***Look at** that strange **man** over there!* (You **look at** something you can see.)
> *I'm **looking for** my diary.* (You **look for** something that you are trying to find.)
> ▶ **talk to / about:**
> *She was **talking to** some **friends**.* (You **talk to** somebody.)
> *They were **talking about** politics.* (You **talk about** something.)

3 In questions that begin with a question word like **What, Who** or **How many**, we usually put the preposition at the end:
> ***Who** are you waiting **for**?*
> ***Who** does this jacket belong **to**?*

4 We do not usually use a preposition after these verbs:

> **phone/ring**: *He **phoned/rang** me last night.* (Not ~~He phoned/rang to me~~ …)
>
> **discuss**: *We often **discuss** sport.* (Not … ~~discuss about sport~~ .)
>
> **answer**: *She didn't **answer** me.* (Not … ~~answer to me~~ .)
>
> **reach** (= arrive): *I **reached** the office at 9 o'clock.* (Not … ~~reached to the office~~ …)

5 Note that we **pay someone**, but we **pay for something**:
> *She paid **him** yesterday.* (You **pay** a person.)
> *I paid **for the books**.* (You **pay for** something that you receive.)
> But note that we **pay** a bill:
> *I'll pay **the bill**.*

···

Practice

A Complete these sentences with the correct prepositions (*to, for*, etc).
In some sentences no preposition is required.

 0 I'm waiting <u>for</u> a telephone call.

 0 We reached <u>—</u> the airport after 11 o'clock.

 1 I'll ask _____ some information.

 2 Let's listen _____ some music.

 3 Where do I pay _____ this shirt?

 4 Let's discuss _____ the arrangements for tomorrow.

 5 Who's going to pay _____ the taxi driver?

 6 We paid _____ the bill and left the restaurant.

 7 I'll phone _____ the theatre and book two tickets.

 8 The price of the holiday depends _____ when you want to travel.

 9 He walked out of the room without answering _____ me.

 10 A lot of people don't agree _____ you.

 11 I've applied _____ a visa.

 12 Who does this pen belong _____ ?

B Complete the story by putting a preposition into the gaps if one is necessary. For some gaps no preposition is required.

> When Jack arrived ^{0} _at_ the theatre, Alice was waiting ^{1}_____
> him. 'Where have you been?' she asked ^{2}_____ him. 'We can talk
> ^{3}_____ that later,' said Jack. 'I tried to phone ^{4}_____ you to
> say that I was going to be late, but you were out. Let's go into the concert.'
> 'OK,' said Alice, 'but you have to pay ^{5}_____ the tickets! The man
> should always pay.' 'I don't agree ^{6}_____ you,' said Jack, 'but I will
> pay if I can. It just depends ^{7}_____ how much they cost. I haven't
> brought much money with me.'

C Complete the questions. The replies will help you. Be careful to put the verbs in the correct tense.

0   A: Who _does this car belong to_ ?
    B: It belongs to the man who lives next door.

1   A: What kind of music do you listen _____?
    B: I listen to classical music and I also listen to some rock.

2   A: What was he _____?
    B: He was talking about his trip to China.

3   A: How many jobs have you _____?
    B: I've applied for five jobs.

4   A: Who _____?
    B: I'm waiting for Mary. We agreed to meet here at 4 o'clock.

5   A: What _____?
    B: I'm looking for my glasses.

6   A: What _____?
    B: She asked for some money.

D Complete the postcard by putting in the prepositions that are necessary. Sometimes, no preposition is required.

> Dear Sam,
> We arrived ^{0} _in_ Greece at about 11 o'clock. We got a taxi from the
> airport to the port, and then we took a lovely, little boat to the island. I
> enjoyed looking ^{1}_____ the scenery on the way. When we reached
> ^{2}_____ the island, we looked ^{3}_____ our villa but we couldn't find it.
> I talked ^{4}_____ a local man, and I asked ^{5}_____ directions. He offered
> to take me there. When we arrived ^{6}_____ the villa, I offered to pay
> ^{7}_____ him, but he didn't want any money. The weather's lovely.
> I'll ring ^{8}_____ you when we get back from our holiday.
> Love,
> Tina

17 Make, do, have, get

1 There are many phrases in which a particular verb is used together with a particular noun, for example:
    make a cup of **coffee**
    do some **work**
    have breakfast

2 We often use **make** in sentences about producing or creating something:
    *They **made** a **fire** in the woods.*
    *Shall I **make** some **coffee**?*
    *He **made** some **sandwiches** for lunch.*

3 We also use **make** in these phrases:
    *Excuse me. I have to **make** a **phone call**.*
    *He **makes** a lot of **mistakes** in his work.*
    *I couldn't sleep because the neighbours were **making** a lot of **noise**.*

4 We often use **do** in sentences about working, or about doing particular jobs:
    *Have you **done** your **homework**?*
    *He offered to **do** the **washing-up**.*
    *We're going to **do** some **shopping**.*
    *I haven't **done** much **work** today.*

5 We use **have** + noun to describe activities:
    *I'm going to **have** a **shower** in the morning.*
    *We usually **have lunch** at about 1 o'clock.*
    *I'm **having fish** for dinner tonight.*
    *I **had** a **swim** in the sea this morning.*

6 We use **get** with adjectives that describe feelings, to say that we begin to have the feeling:
    *I'm **getting tired** now. I need a rest.*
    *They're late and I'm **getting worried**.*
    *I **got angry** and shouted at them.*

7 We use **get** in some phrases that describe a change of situation:
    *We **got lost** in Paris. (= We became lost …)*
    *It's **getting cold**. (= It's becoming cold.)*
    *Jane was very ill, but she's **getting better**.*
    *They **got married** three years ago.*
    *It rained heavily and I **got** very **wet**.*

8 We use **make** + someone + **adjective** to talk about the cause of a feeling:
    *He **made us** very **angry**.*
    *The news **made him happy**.*

Practice

A Complete the sentences, using the correct forms of *make, do, have* or *get*. Be careful that you use the correct tense.

0 He was __making__ a cup of coffee in the kitchen.

0 We __had__ lunch in a very pleasant little restaurant yesterday.

1 She always _____ excited before her birthday.

2 A: Helen's ill.

    B: Oh dear. I hope she will _____ better soon.

3 We have to _____ some homework every evening.

4 I think I've _____ a terrible mistake.

5 They _____ the shopping and then they went home.

6 I was late because I _____ lost on my way there.

7 It always _____ very hot here during the summer.

8 Could I _____ a quick phone call, please?

9 Please don't _____ so much noise.

10 It was a lovely surprise and it _____ me very happy.

11 Her parents are _____ old. They are sixty or seventy.

12 How old were you when you _____ married?

B **Look at the notes in the box about what Laura did yesterday. Complete the sentences, using the correct forms of *make, do, have* or *get*. Sometimes more than one answer is possible.**

7.30	Got up. Shower.
8.00	Breakfast. (fruit juice and toast)
8.30 – 9.00	Walk to work. Rain.
9.00 – 1.00	Work. Very busy.
1.00 – 2.00	Lunch in office. Sandwiches.
2.00 – 5.00	Work. Finished everything.
5.30	Shopping. Home.
7.00	Pizza for dinner. Washed up.
8.00 – 11.00	TV. Tired. Bed.

It was a normal day for Laura yesterday. She got up at 7.30 and she

⁰ had_____ a shower. Then she ¹_____ breakfast. For breakfast

she ²_____ cornflakes and toast. While she was walking to work, it

rained and she ³_____ wet. She ⁴_____ angry about this. In

the morning she ⁵_____ a lot of work. She ⁶_____ lunch at

about 1 o'clock. She ⁷_____ sandwiches for lunch. When she had

⁸_____ all her work in the afternoon, she went home. On the way

home she ⁹_____ some shopping.

She ¹⁰_____ a pizza for dinner. She ¹¹_____ the washing-up

and then she watched TV for three hours. By eleven o'clock she felt quite

tired, and so she went to bed.

C **Complete the dialogues, using the correct form of *make, do, have* or *get*.**

0   A: Was the film good?

    B: No, I _got_____ bored in the middle of it.

1   A: Could you _____ some shopping for me?

    B: Yes, what do you want me to buy?

2   A: Were you pleased by the news?

    B: No, it _____ me very unhappy.

3   A: Was it a warm day?

    B: Yes, but it _____ rather cold in the evening.

4   A: Are you hungry at the moment?

    B: No, I _____ a big meal a couple of hours ago.

5   A: Did he pass the test?

    B: No, he _____ a lot of mistakes.

6   A: Are you ready to go out?

    B: No, I'm not. I want to _____ a wash first.

7   A: Could you repair this for me?

    B: Yes, but I can't _____ the job until tomorrow.

18 Word order: subject, verb, object etc.

1 Look at this table:

SUBJECT	+ VERB	+ OBJECT
Our firm	makes	computers.
I	posted	the letter.
She	caught	the train.
The phone	doesn't work.	
He	was eating	a sandwich.

Sentences must have a subject and a verb.
If there is an object, it usually goes after the
verb. Any other information, such as a time,
a place etc, usually follows the object:

SUBJECT	+ VERB	+ OBJECT	+ PLACE
She	met	Tom	in Rome.

(Not ~~She met in Rome Tom.~~)

2 We put an adjective before a noun:

	ARTICLE	+ ADJECTIVE	+ NOUN
She has	a	blue	dress.

We put an adjective after **be**, **get**, and **seem**:

	VERB	+ ADJECTIVE
She	**is**	clever.
He	**seems**	nice.

3 We usually put a place before a time:

	+ PLACE	+ TIME
He worked	in a factory	for a year.
They've been	here	since 2.
We met	in France	last June.
I walked	around the town	yesterday.

4 We usually put a direction before a time:

	+ DIRECTION	+ TIME
The bus arrived	from Liverpool	at 10.30.
He came	to this country	in 1985.
They moved	into the flat	yesterday.

5 Look at the word order in these questions:

VERB+	SUBJECT	+ VERB	+ OBJECT
When did	you	join	the club?
			+ PLACE
Can	you	come	here?
			+ DIRECTION
When are	you	going	to the USA?
			+ TIME
What are	you	doing	tonight?

....

Practice

A Put the words in brackets ( ) into the correct order to make a sentence.

0 (me – she – at half past 4 – phoned)

    <u>She phoned me at half past 4.</u>

1 (my coat – where – you – put – did – ?)

    _____

2 (from the airport – took – we – a taxi)

    _____

3 (three weeks ago – the job – started – she)

    _____

4 (around Europe – last summer – travelled – two friends and I)

    _____

5 (tomorrow – you – to Italy – going – are – ?)

    _____

6 (Egypt – you – when – did – visit – ?)

    _____

B **Write the story by putting the words and phrases into the right order.**

0 (came – at 7.30 this morning – the postman)

   The postman came at 7.30 this morning.

1 (he – a letter – brought)

   _____

2 (It – a letter from Maria and her son Matthew – was)

   _____

3 I – before I went to work – read – it)

   _____

4 (they – here – next week – are coming)

   _____

5 (at the airport – them – on Tuesday – I – am going to meet)

   _____

6 (at my house – are going to stay – they)

   _____

7 (takes – abroad – her son – every year – she)

   _____

8 (him – last year – took – she – to France)

   _____

9 (next year – her – am going to visit – I)

   _____

C **Complete this job interview by putting in Mr Jones' questions.**

Mr Jones: 0 _Have you done this kind of work_   before?

Miss Smith: No, I haven't done this kind of work.

Mr Jones: Where 1_____ the advertisement?

Miss Smith: I saw it in the local newspaper.

Mr Jones: Do 2_____?

Miss Smith: No, I don't speak any foreign languages

Mr Jones: Where 3_____ at the moment?

Miss Smith: I'm working in a travel agent's at the moment.

Mr Jones: When 4_____?

Miss Smith: I started there two years ago.

Mr Jones: Can 5_____?

Miss Smith: Yes, I can use a computer.

Mr Jones: 6_____?

Miss Smith: Yes, I like the job.

Mr Jones: Why 7_____?

Miss Smith   I'm leaving because I want to earn more money.

Mr Jones: 8_____?

Miss Smith: I can start next month.

19 Who? and What?: subject and object questions

1 Compare these examples:

SUBJECT
Ann: | Who | **told** you?
Mary: *James told me.*

This is a subject question.

OBJECT
Ann: | Who | **did** you **tell**?
Mary: *I told Bill.*

This is an object question.

2 Compare subject and object questions with **Who**:

In the sentence ***Who told you?***, **Who** is the subject. Here is another example:

SUBJECT
Ann: | Who | **wrote** Hamlet?
(= **Somebody** wrote *Hamlet*. Who?)
Mary: *Shakespeare wrote Hamlet.*

When **Who** is the subject, the order of the words is the same as in a statement:

SUBJECT
Who | **is going** to come with me?
Who | **lives** in that old house?
Who | **wants** some more coffee?

In the sentence ***Who did you tell?***, **Who** is the object. Here is another example:

OBJECT
Ann: | Who | **did** you **meet** last night?
(= You met **somebody**. Who?)
Mary: *I met a couple of friends.*

When **Who** is the object, we use an auxiliary (**be**, **do**, **have** etc.) before the subject:

OBJECT
Who | **are** you **going** to invite?
Who | **did** Laura **ask** for help?
Who | **have** you **told** about this?

3 Compare subject and object questions with **What**:

SUBJECT
What | **is** in this dish?
(= **Something** is in it. What?)

OBJECT
What | **did** you **buy** at the shops?
(= You bought **something**. What?)

Practice

A **Write questions beginning with *Who* or *What* from the sentences in brackets ().**

0 (Eric met **somebody**.) _Who did Eric meet?_

0 (**Somebody** ate the last piece of cake.) _Who ate the last piece of cake?_

1 (**Somebody** wants some more coffee.) _____

2 (**Something** happened at the end of the story.) _____

3 (**Somebody** is going to pay the bill.) _____

4 (He had **something** for breakfast.) _____

5 (Their letter said **something**.) _____

6 (**Somebody** knows the answer to my question.) _____

7 (They saw **something**.) _____

8 (She is phoning **somebody**.) _____

B Use the 'full' answers to write questions using *Who* or *What*. (We usually use the short, <u>underlined</u> answers when we reply to a question.)

QUESTIONS

ANSWERS

0 <u>Who were you talking to on the phone</u> ? ~ (I was talking to) **Elizabeth** (on the phone).

0 <u>What was the result of the game</u> ? ~ (The result of the game was) **2–0 to Italy** .

1 _____ ? ~ **Anita and Frank** (went on the trip).

2 _____ ? ~ **I'm not sure** (what's happening in this film).

3 _____ ? ~ (I'm going to phone) **Jane** .

4 _____ ? ~ (I watched) **that new comedy programme** (on TV last night).

5 _____ ? ~ **John** (sent these flowers).

6 _____ ? ~ (I bought) **a book** (in that shop).

7 _____ ? ~ **Some good news** (has made Tom so happy).

C Read this story and then complete the questions.

Two days ago Robert took his driving test. He failed it. Afterwards he met his friend Philip. He told Philip that he had failed his test. Then he said, 'Don't tell anyone. It's a secret.' Philip said, 'OK, I won't tell anyone.'

Later that day, Philip met Linda for coffee and he said, 'Robert failed his driving test.' Linda laughed. 'Poor Robert,' she said.

QUESTIONS

ANSWERS

0 (What / Robert / do / two days ago?)
   <u>What did Robert do two days ago?</u> ~ He took his driving test.

1 (What / happen?)
   _____ ~ He failed it.

2 (Who / take / his / driving test?)
   _____ ~ Robert.

3 (What / Robert / fail?)
   _____ ~ His driving test.

4 (Who / Robert / meet / afterwards?)
   _____ ~ He met Philip.

5 (What / Robert / say / to Philip?)
   _____ ~ He said, 'Don't tell anyone.'

6 (What / Philip / say / to Robert?)
   _____ ~ Philip said, 'OK, I won't tell anyone.'

7 (Who / Philip / meet / for coffee?)
   _____ ~ He met Linda.

8 (What / Philip / say / to Linda?)
   _____ ~ He said, 'Robert failed his driving test.'

9 (What / Linda / do?)
   _____ ~ She laughed.

20 How long? How far? How often? How much? etc.

1 We use **How long ...?** to ask about a period of time:
 > **How long** have you been waiting? ~ About 20 minutes.
 > **How long** will the journey take? ~ Three hours.

 We use **from ... to** or **from ... until** to talk about a period of time:
 > She was a student **from** 1985 **to** 1990.
 > Tomorrow I'm working **from** 8.30 **until** 6.

2 We use **How far ...?** to ask about the distance from one place to another. We can use **from** and **to** with the places we are asking about:
 > **How far** is it **from** Amsterdam **to** Paris? ~ 475 kilometres.
 > **How far** are the shops **from** here? ~ Not far.

3 We use **How often ...?** to ask about the number of times something happens. We can use phrases like **every day, once a week** etc. in the answer:
 > **How often** do the buses run? ~ **Every hour**.
 > **How often** do you play squash? ~ **Twice a week**.

4 We can use **How much ...?** to ask about the price of something:
 > **How much** is a return ticket to Florence?
 > **How much** did you pay for this car?

5 We use **How much ...?** with an uncountable noun to ask about the amount of something. An uncountable noun cannot be plural because it describes something that cannot be counted (e.g. **bread, work, weather, money, music, meat, milk, cheese**).
 > **How much bread** is there in the cupboard?
 > **How much work** have you done today?

6 We use **How many ...?** with a plural noun to ask about numbers:
 > **How many students** are in your class? ~ 15.
 > **How many people** went to the party? ~ Ten.

7 We use **How old ...?** to ask about someone's age:
 > **How old** are you? ~ I'm 19.
 > Note that we say:
 > I am 19, or: 19. (Not ~~I have 19.~~)
 > We can also say: I'm 19 years old.
 > But we cannot say: ~~I'm 19 years.~~

....

Practice

A Complete the questions using *How long, How old, How often* etc. Put the verbs into the correct tense.

QUESTIONS

0 (How / you / stay / in New Zealand?)
 <u>How long did you stay in New Zealand?</u>

1 (How / he / read / a newspaper?)
 _____

2 (How / a single room / cost?)
 _____

3 (How / be / you when you went to live in Australia?)
 _____

4 (How / exams / you / going to take?)
 _____

5 (How / the course / last?)
 _____

6 (How / be / it from here to the nearest bus stop?)
 _____

ANSWERS

~ I stayed there for six months.

~ He reads one every day.

~ It costs £50 a night.

~ I was 15 when I went there.

~ I'm going to take three exams.

~ It will last for two years.

~ It's about 200 metres.

B Make each question using the words in brackets ( ), and *How old,*
   How much, How many etc. Put the verbs into the correct tense.

0 A: <u>How old is your husband</u> (your husband/be)?
   B: He is 34. He'll be 35 next month.

1 A: _____ (languages you/speak)?
   B: I speak three – English, French and Chinese.

2 A: _____ (it/be) from here to the airport?
   B: It's about 25 kilometres.

3 A: _____ (the meal/cost)?
   B: I can't remember, but it wasn't very expensive.

4 A: _____ (you/stay) there?
   B: I stayed there from June until October.

5 A: _____ (the postman/come)?
   B: He comes twice a day.

6 A: _____ (cheese/you/buy)?
   B: I bought half a kilo.

C Complete each of these sentences by putting one word into each gap.

0 It was my birthday last week. I <u>am</u> 21.
1 The programme lasts _____ 8.30 _____ 10 o'clock.
2 There is a train to the centre _____ 30 minutes in the morning.
3 How _____ money have you got?
4 How far is it _____ here _____ the city centre?
5 My grandfather is seventy _____ _____ .
6 How _____ countries have you visited?

D Complete the conversation by putting in Bob's questions. Start with *How ...* each time.

Anne: I'm doing a course in computing.
Bob: Oh really. 0 <u>How long have you been doing it</u> ?
Anne: I've been doing it for about a month. It's at the local college.
Bob: 1 _____ ?
Anne: I go there twice a week.
Bob: 2 _____ ?
Anne: The lessons last for three hours, from 2 o'clock until 5.
Bob: 3 _____ ?
Anne: I study at home every evening.
Bob: 4 _____ ?
Anne: There are about 25 people in my class.

Bob: 5 _____ ?
Anne: They're all about the same age as me.
Bob: 6 _____ ?
Anne It's not far from my home.
Bob: 7 _____ ?
Anne: It doesn't cost anything. My company is paying.

21 Question tags (**It's cold, isn't it?**)

1 A question tag is a short question (e.g. **isn't it?**, **haven't we?**) that we can add at the end of a statement:

Henry: *We've met before, **haven't we?***

Jeff: *Yes, we have.*

2 Look at this bit of a conversation:

Anna: *Sandra is Swiss.*

David: *No, she's French, **isn't she?***
(= I thought she was French, but am I wrong?)

When tag questions really are questions, like David's, the voice goes up at the end.

But when tag questions are not really questions, the voice goes down at the end:

*That was a boring programme, **wasn't it?***
(= I think that was a boring programme.)

3 Note that the verb we use in the tag depends on the verb used in the statement:

VERB		+ TAG
be:	*You're French,*	***aren't you?***
verb:	*He **plays** golf,*	***doesn't he?***
auxiliary verb:	*It **has** arrived,*	***hasn't it?***

4 A positive statement has a negative tag:

POSITIVE + NEGATIVE	
I'm right,	***aren't I?***
	(Not ~~amn't I?~~)
You're 18,	***aren't you?***
They're getting tired,	***aren't they?***
They were friendly,	***weren't they?***
He lives in France	***doesn't he?***
You speak Spanish,	***don't you?***
You passed your exams,	***didn't you?***
She has left,	***hasn't she?***
You can drive,	***can't you?***
The bus will come soon,	***won't it?***

5 A negative statement has a positive tag:

NEGATIVE + POSITIVE	
It isn't very cheap,	***is it?***
We aren't going to be late,	***are we?***
She wasn't angry,	***was she?***
You don't like this,	***do you?***
She didn't win,	***did she?***
She hasn't visited Ireland,	***has she?***
She can't drive,	***can she?***
It won't rain today,	***will it?***

....

Practice

A   Complete the conversation by putting in question tags.

Tim: We haven't met before, **⁰ have we**   ?

Jo: No, I've just arrived in this country.

Tim: You come from Australia, ¹_____ ?

Jo: Yes, from Sydney.

Tim: It's very hot there, ²_____ ?

Jo: Most of the time, but not always.

Tim: But it never gets very cold, ³_____ ?

Jo: No, well, not as cold as some places.

Tim: They speak English there, ⁴_____ ?

Jo: Yes, that's right.

Tim: You haven't been here long, ⁵_____ ?

Jo: No, I only got here two weeks ago.

Tim: You're on holiday, ⁶_____ ?

Jo: Yes, I'm travelling around for six months.

B **Complete the sentences by putting in question tags.**

0 The programme starts at 7 o'clock, _doesn't it_____ ? ~ Yes, that's right.

1 I can use this ticket on any bus, _____ ? ~ Yes, you can.

2 The bill won't be very high, _____ ? ~ No, I don't think so.

3 He wasn't very polite, _____ ? ~ No, he wasn't.

4 I didn't make a mistake, _____ ? ~ No, you didn't.

5 It won't be a difficult thing to do, _____ ? ~ No, I don't think so.

6 That was a lovely meal, _____ ? ~ Yes, it was delicious.

7 You can't play the piano, _____ ? ~ No, I can't.

8 They left last week, _____ ? ~ Yes, that's right.

C **Complete the conversation with question tags.**

Marta: I'm going to Helsinki tomorrow.

Charles: That's in Finland, [1]_____ ?

Marta: Yes, it's the capital.

Charles: You've been there before, [2]_____ ?

Marta: Yes, two years ago.

Charles: But you can't speak Finnish, [3]_____ ?

Marta: No, I can't.

Charles: But a lot of Finnish people speak English, [4]_____ ?

Marta: Yes.

Charles: Well, I'll see you before you leave, [5]_____ ?

Marta: Yes, I'll see you tonight.

D **Complete the sentence with a question tag before each reply.**

0 A: She _comes from Italy, doesn't she?_____

   B: Yes, she comes from Italy.

1 A: You can _____

   B: Yes, I can speak French very well.

2 A: You haven't _____

   B: No, I haven't heard this story.

3 A: You went _____

   B: Yes, I went to Frank's party.

4 A: It isn't _____

   B: No, it isn't very far from here.

5 A: She won't _____

   B: No, she won't be angry.

6 A: You're not _____

   B: No, I'm not going to leave now.

7 A: You'll _____

   B: Yes, I'll be at home tonight.

22 Must, mustn't (I must leave)

1 We use **must** with an infinitive (**do, go, work**, etc.):

INFINITIVE

You must **work** *harder.*

Don't use **to** before the infinitive:
Not ~~You must to work harder.~~

The form of **must** is the same for all persons:

| I/you/he/she/it/we/they **must leave** soon. |

2 We use **must** in rules, to say that an action is necessary:

All visitors **must go** *to reception when they arrive.*

We use **You must** … to give somebody an order:

Your work is poor – **you must try** *harder.*
You must finish *this work tomorrow.*

We use **I/We must** … to say that we think it is necessary that we do something:

I'm getting tired. **I must go** *home now.*
We must get *a new car soon.*

3 We also use **You must** … to strongly recommend or offer something:

You must read *this book; it's fantastic!*
You must come *for lunch at our house.*

4 The negative form of **must** is **mustn't** or **must not**:

You **mustn't park** *here – it's not allowed.*
Not ~~You mustn't to park here.~~

5 We use **You mustn't** … (or **You must not**) to say that it is necessary that somebody does NOT do something:

You **mustn't smoke** *in here.*
You **mustn't make** *this mistake again.*

We use **I/We mustn't** … (or **must not**) to say that we think it is necessary that we do NOT do something:

I **mustn't forget** *her birthday again.*
We **mustn't be** *late for the meeting.*

6 Notice that we can use **must** and **mustn't** (not ~~will must~~) to talk about the future:

I **must** *phone Harry tomorrow.*
(Not ~~I will must phone …~~)

To talk about what was necessary in the past, we cannot use **must**; we use a form of **have to** (see unit 23).

We don't generally use **must** in a question form. We use **have to** (see unit 23).

···

Practice

A The 'Hotel Strict' is not a very nice hotel. It has a lot of rules. Read the list of rules, and change each one into a sentence using *must* or *must not*.

> **Notice to guests**
> Leave your key at reception when you go out.
> Do not take food into your room.
> Pay for your room when you arrive.
> Vacate your room by 9 a.m. on the day you leave.
> Do not smoke in the restaurant.
> Return to the hotel before 10 o'clock every night.

0   You must leave _____ your key at reception when you go out.

1   You _____ food into your room.

2   _____ for your room when you arrive.

3   _____ your room by 9 a.m. on the day you leave.

4   _____ in the restaurant.

5   _____ to the hotel before 10 o'clock every night.

B Complete the sentences with *must* or *mustn't* and the verb in brackets.

0 You __must hear_____ (hear) this story; it's extremely funny!

1 We _____ (forget) to buy some petrol. There isn't much left.

2 I _____ (go) to the shops this afternoon. I've got no food in the house.

3 You _____ (worry) so much; it's bad for you.

4 We _____ (book) the tickets before it's too late.

5 You _____ (lock) the door with this key every time you go out.

6 You _____ (see) that new, French film. It's really good.

7 I _____ (phone) Jane tonight. She asked me to call her.

C Look at this table of instructions for students in a school. Use the table to make sentences with *must* or *mustn't*.

	Yes	No
Attend all classes.	✓	
Take school books home with you.		✓
Make a noise in the corridors.		✓
Write in school books.		✓
Arrive for lessons on time.	✓	
Bring your own pens and paper.	✓	

0 __You must attend_____ all classes.

1 _____ school books home with you.

2 _____ a noise in the corridors.

3 _____ in school books.

4 _____ for lessons on time.

5 _____ your own pens and paper.

D Rewrite the sentences in brackets using *must* or *mustn't* / *must not*.

0 (Have some of this fish. It's wonderful.)
   You __must have some of this fish__. It's wonderful.

1 (Don't tell lies. It's bad.)
   You _____. It's bad.

2 (Passengers: Do not open the door while the train is moving.)
   Passengers _____ while the train is moving.

3 (Come for dinner with us one evening next week!)
   You _____ one evening next week!

4 (All staff: Show identity cards when you enter the building.)
   All staff _____ when they enter the building.

5 (It's bad for you to eat so much unhealthy food.)
   You _____ so much unhealthy food.

6 (Follow the instructions when using this machine.)
   You _____ when using this machine.

7 (It's important that I write this letter today.)
   I _____ this letter today.

23 Have to (He has to go)

1 The Present Simple forms of **have to** are:

POSITIVE & NEGATIVE		
I/you/we/they	{ **have** / **don't have** }	} to go.
He/she/it	{ **has** / **doesn't have** }	

QUESTIONS			
Do	I/you/we/they	} **have**	to go?
Does	he/she/it		

2 We use **have to** to talk about things that are necessary because of rules that other people oblige us to follow:

My brother **has to travel** a lot in his job.
(It is required by his employer.)
We **have to pay** the rent every month.
(It is required by the landlord.)

To talk about things that WE think are necessary, we usually use **must** (see unit 22).

3 We also use **have to** for things that are necessary because of the circumstances:

I **have to get** a bus to school. (It is the only way I can travel there.)
She **has to live** on a small income. (She only receives a small amount of money to pay for what she needs.)

4 We use **don't have to** to say that something is NOT necessary:

We **don't have to hurry**; we're early. (= It's not necessary to hurry. We have plenty of time.)
I **don't have to get** up early on Sunday. I can stay in bed if I want.

5 We form the past of **have to** like this:

I **had to do** a lot of work yesterday.
We **didn't have to play** football at school.
Did you **have to work** hard for the exam?

6 We form the future of **have to** like this:

He'**ll have to look** for another job.
We **won't have to get** tickets in advance.
Will they **have to get** visas?

Note that we can use the Present Simple of **have to** to talk about the future:

I **have to do** some shopping tomorrow.
Do you **have to work** next weekend?

··

Practice

A Look at this table about different jobs and use the information to complete the sentences, using *have to* or *don't have to*.

	Shop Assistants	Bank clerks	Doctors	Teachers
deal with the public	✓	✓	✓	✗
be polite to people	✓	✓	✗	✗
work with money	✓	✓	✗	✗
wear uniforms	✓	✗	✓	✗

0 Shop assistants <u>have to deal with</u> the public.

1 Teachers ——————————— the public.

2 Teachers ——————————— to people.

3 Bank clerks ——————————— to people.

4 Shop assistants ——————————— with money.

5 Bank clerks ——————————— with money.

6 Doctors ——————————— with money.

7 Shop assistants often ——————————— uniforms.

8 Teachers ——————————— uniforms.

B Complete the sentences using the correct forms of *have to* and
the words in brackets. Be careful to use the correct tense.

0 <u>I have to leave</u>   (I/leave) now; I've got an appointment at the dentist's.

0 <u>Did you have to study</u>   (you/study) literature when you were at school?

0 <u>You don't have to come</u>   (You/not/come) with me now if you don't want to.

1 _____ (I/not/work) hard because the job was very easy.

2 _____ (I/do) this work now, or can I do it tomorrow?

3 _____ (I/run) to school because I was late.

4 _____ (I/go) to an important meeting yesterday.

5 _____ (you/show) your passports when you reached the border?

6 _____ (I/pay) in cash next week or can I give you a cheque?

7 I want to be an airline pilot. What qualifications _____ (you/have)
to be a pilot?

8 _____ (You/not/decide) today. You can tell me tomorrow.

9 I arrived late yesterday because _____ (I/wait) a long time for a bus.

10 A: _____ (you/work) every weekend?

    B: No, I don't; but _____ (I/work) last weekend.

C Complete the conversations, using the correct forms of *have to*.

A: (Good morning, I'd like to buy a travel card. What / I / do?)

    0 <u>Good morning. I'd like to buy a travel card. What do I have to do?</u>

B: (You / fill / in an application form.)

    1 _____

A: (I/ give / you / a photograph?)

    2 _____

B: (No, you / not / give / me anything, except the money for the card!)

    3 _____

Dad: (What / you / do / at school today?)

        0 <u>What did you have to do at school today?</u>

Geoff: (We / do / some / English tests.)

        4 _____

Dad: (How many questions / you / answer?)

        5 _____

Geoff: (We / answer / about 40 grammar questions.)

        6 _____

        (I / think / about them very carefully.)

        7 _____

Dad: (you / write / a composition?)

        8 _____

Geoff: (No, but we / do / one next week.)

        9 _____

24 Should, shouldn't (You shouldn't smoke)

1 We use **should** with an infinitive (**do**, **go** etc.):

INFINITIVE

I **should** do some work tonight.

The form of **should** is the same for all persons:

I/you/he/she/it/we/they **should go.**

2 The negative form is **shouldn't**:
You **shouldn't sit** in the sun all day.
They **shouldn't spend** so much money.

3 We use **I should** or **we should** to say what is a good thing for us to do:
I **should go** home. It's midnight.
We **should invite** them for a meal.

We use **I** or **we shouldn't** to say that something is a bad thing for us to do:
I **shouldn't spend** so much money.

We use **you should/shouldn't** to give advice:
You **should look** for a better job.
You **shouldn't drive** so fast.

Should is not as strong as **must** or **have to**. Compare:
You **should eat** more fruit. (It's a good idea.)
'You **must eat** more fruit,' said the doctor. (It's very important).

4 We use the question form **should I/we ...?** to ask for advice:

Should I write my name in this space?

What **should** I **say** to Helen?
I need a new passport. Where **should** I **go**?

5 We can say **I think we should, I don't think you should** etc. to give an opinion:

I think we should get a new car.

I **don't think you should believe** everything he says.
We do not usually say:
~~I think you shouldn't ...~~

6 We can use **do you think I should ...?** to ask for advice:
He hasn't replied to my letter. **Do you think I should phone** him?
What **do you think** I **should give** Tom for his birthday?

Practice

A Complete the sentences, using *should* or *shouldn't* and the words in brackets.

0 You shouldn't work _____ (You/work) so hard. Have a holiday.

0 I enjoyed that film. We should go _____ (We/go) to the cinema more often.

1 _____ (You/park) here. It's not allowed.

2 What _____ (I/cook) for dinner tonight?

3 _____ (You/wear) a coat. It's cold outside.

4 _____ (You/smoke). It's bad for you.

5 _____ (We/arrive) at the airport two hours before the flight.

6 _____ (I/pay) now or later?

7 Do you think _____ (I/apply) for this job?

8 What do you think _____ (I/write) in this space on the form?

9 _____ (I/eat) any more cake. I've already eaten too much.

10 This food is terrible. _____ (We/complain) to the manager.

11 Which shirt do you think _____ (I/buy) ?

B Henry is cooking a meal. Give him some useful advice. Use *you should* or *you shouldn't* and the notes in the box.

> Don't leave the meat in the oven for more than one hour.
> Cut the onions as small as possible.
> Use fresh herbs and fresh vegetables.
> Don't put in too much salt and pepper.
> Wait until the water boils before you put the vegetables into it.
> Heat the oven before you put the meat in.
> Cut the meat into four equal slices.

0 You shouldn't leave _____ the meat in the oven for more than one hour.

1 _____ the onions as small as possible.

2 _____ fresh herbs and fresh vegetables.

3 _____ in too much salt and pepper.

4 _____ until the water boils before you put the vegetables into it.

5 _____ the oven before you put the meat in.

6 _____ the meat into four equal slices.

C Write this conversation between Brian and Keith using the words in brackets. Put in *do* or *should* where required.

Brian: (I want to buy a motorbike. What / you / think / I / do?)

   0 I want to buy a motorbike. What *do* you think I *should* do?

Keith: (You / look / at the advertisements in the papers.)

   0 You should look at the advertisements in the papers.

Brian: (Which papers / I / get?)

   1 _____

Keith: (I think / you / buy / the local newspapers.)

   2 _____

Brian: (What / you / think / I / do / before I buy a bike?)

   3 _____

Keith: (I / not / think / you / decide / too quickly.)

   4 _____

   (You / check / the condition of the bike.)

   5 _____

   (You / ask / somebody who knows about bikes to look at the bike for you.)

   6 _____

   (You / not / buy / one simply because it looks nice!)

   7 _____

   (You / be / very careful.)

   8 _____

25 Can, could; may, might

1 We use **can** or **could** with an infinitive (**do**, **speak**, **swim** etc.):

> I/you/he (etc.) **can** | INFINITIVE **swim** | to the island.

2 Look at these examples with **can**:

> ABILITY:
> I **can speak** four languages.
> (= I am able to speak four languages.)
> **Can** you **swim**?
> (= Are you able to swim?)

We use **can** to talk about what people are able to do.

In the negative, we use **can't** or **cannot** to talk about what people are not able to do:
> Please speak slowly. I **can't** understand you.
> (= I am not able to understand you.)
> Robert **can't run** as fast as Sarah.
> We **can't go** abroad for our holiday this year, because we **cannot afford** the air fare.

We use **could** and **couldn't** to talk about what people were able to do in the past:
> When Jane was little, she **could swim** before she **could walk**.
> I **couldn't answer** every question in the test.
> I **couldn't go** to their party. I was ill.

3 We use **may** or **might** with an infinitive (**do**, **go**, **leave** etc.):

> I/you/he/we (etc.) **may** | INFINITIVE **leave** | soon.

4 Look at these examples with **may** and **might**:

> POSSIBILITY:
> The letter **may come** tomorrow.
> (= It's possible that the letter will come tomorrow.)
> Ask Eric. He **might know** the answer.
> (= Perhaps Eric knows the answer.)

We use **may** or **might** to talk about things that are possible, now or in the future.

The negative is **may not** or **might not**:
> I'll phone her, but she **may not be** at home.
> (= It's possible that she isn't at home.)
> I **might not go** to work tomorrow. (= It's possible that I won't go to work tomorrow.)

Note that we can use the short form **mightn't**, but we do not say ~~mayn't~~:
> She **mightn't be** at home now.
> I **mightn't go** to work tomorrow.

....

Practice

A   Complete the sentences with *can, can't* or *couldn't* and the verbs in brackets ().

0   You don't have to shout. I ___can hear_____ (hear) you very well.

0   I ___couldn't watch_____ (watch) that programme last night because I had to go out.

1   He _____ (play) last week because he was injured.

2   He eats in restaurants all the time because he _____ (cook) .

3   I _____ (give) you a lift in my car because it isn't working at the moment.

4   I didn't have a good seat in the theatre, so I _____ (see) the stage very well.

5   John doesn't need a calculator. He _____ (do) very difficult sums in his head.

6   She's very good at music. She _____ (play) three instruments.

7   I _____ (find) my address book. Have you seen it?

8   He spoke very quickly and I _____ (understand) anything he said.

9   We _____ (go) on the trip because we _____ (afford) it. It was very expensive.

10 I _____ (do) any more work because I was very tired, so I stopped.

11 I'm afraid that I _____ (talk) to you now. I'm in a hurry. I have to be at work in five minutes.

B **Use the words in brackets to complete each sentence, with *can, can't, could* or *couldn't*.**

0 Sarah phoned Jane yesterday. (They / not / talk / for a long time, because Jane had to go out.)
   They _couldn't talk for a long time, because Jane had to go out._

1 Grandma needs her glasses. (She / not / see / anything without her glasses.)
   She _____

2 Mary won her race. (She was so tired after the race that she / not / stand / up.)
   She _____

3 (Last year, Robert / beat / his younger brother at chess.) But he can't beat him now.
   Last year, _____

4 John and Anna have a wonderful view from their hotel room. (They / see / the whole of the city.)
   They _____

C **Complete the sentences, using *might* or *might not* and the verb in brackets.**

0 Accept their offer. You _might not get_ (get) a better opportunity.

1 I _____ (buy) her this plant for her birthday. She likes plants a lot.

2 Take a coat with you. It _____ (be) cold this evening.

3 We _____ (go) to Greece this summer, but we haven't booked anything yet.

4 I _____ (go) by car because there will be a lot of traffic.

5 They _____ (come) to the party tonight. They're very busy. They have a lot of things to do at home.

6 A: What are you going to do tonight?
   B: I'm not sure. I _____ (stay) at home. I'm tired.

7 I know Jane is at school today. But I don't know where she is at the moment. She _____ (be) in the gym, or she _____ (be) in the science lab.

8 Don't worry too much about that mistake. It _____ (be) important.

9 I'll try to change the time of my flight, but it _____ (be) possible. The planes are often full at this time of year.

10 You _____ (find) a good hotel if you go to the main street — there are lots of hotels there.

D **Complete the conversation using *may* or *may not* and the verbs in brackets.**

Jane: Are you going to the concert tomorrow?

Chris: I ⁰ _may go_ (go), but there ¹ _____ (be) any tickets left.

Jane: What will you do if you can't go to the concert?

Chris: I'm not sure. I ² _____ (go) out at all. I ³ _____ (stay) at home. I ⁴ _____ (watch) a video.

Jane: What kind of film will you get?

Chris: I don't know. I ⁵ _____ (get) a horror film. I like them!

26 Passive: Present Simple and Past Simple

1 We form the Present Simple passive like this:

am/is/are + PAST PARTICIPLE		
Glass	*is*	*made* *from sand.*

POSITIVE & NEGATIVE
*This programme **is shown** on TV every Thursday.*
*These computers **aren't produced** any more.*

QUESTIONS
*When **is** breakfast **served** in this hotel?*

(For information on the forms of regular past participles, see Table D on page 95, and for irregular past participles, see Table E on page 96.)

2 We form the Past Simple passive like this:

was/were + PAST PARTICIPLE		
Anna	*was*	*born* *in Germany.*

POSITIVE & NEGATIVE
*'Romeo and Juliet' **was written** by Shakespeare.*
*The goods **weren't delivered** yesterday.*

QUESTIONS
*When **was** your camera stolen?*

3 Look at these sentences:

ACTIVE: *They sell* OBJECT *cold drinks here.*

PASSIVE: SUBJECT *Cold drinks are sold here.*

Notice that the object in the active sentence (**cold drinks**) is the same as the subject in the passive sentence. We use the passive when it is not important who does the action, or when we don't know who does it:
These cars are made in Japan. (We don't need to say ~~... by Japanese workers.~~)
This castle was built in the twelfth century. (We don't know who built it.)

4 Now look at these examples:
(i) ***Alfred Hitchcock** was a great film maker. **He** directed this film in 1956.*
(ii) *This is a wonderful **film**. **It** was directed by Alfred Hitchcock.*
In (ii) we use the passive because we have been talking about something (**the film**), and not the person who did it (**Hitchcock**). We use **by** to say who does, or did, the action:
*This film was directed **by Hitchcock.***

··

Practice

A Complete these sentences with the Present Simple passive form of the verbs in brackets ( ).

0   English _is spoken_____ (speak) in many countries.

1   The post _____ (deliver) at about 7 o'clock every morning.

2   Dinner _____ (serve) in the hotel at 8.30 p.m.

3   The building _____ (not/use) any more.

4   The Olympic Games _____ (hold) every 4 years.

5   How _____ (your name/spell) ?

6   What kinds of things _____ (sell) in that market?

7   My salary _____ (pay) every month.

8   These computers _____ (make) in Japan.

9   The rubbish _____ (take) away three times a week.

10   The name of the person who committed the crime _____ (not know) .

11   This programme _____ (show) three times a week.

12   His travel expenses _____ (pay) by his company.

B Complete these sentences using the Past Simple passive form of the verbs in brackets.

0 My car _was repaired_____ (repair) last week.

1 This song _____ (write) by John Lennon and Paul McCartney.

2 The phone _____ (answer) by a young girl.

3 The film _____ (make) ten years ago.

4 When _____ (tennis/invent) ?

5 She _____ (not/injure) in the accident.

6 He _____ (be born) in 1965.

7 Where _____ (this pot/make) ?

8 When _____ (this city/build) ?

9 This picture _____ (paint) by Picasso.

10 When _____ (this book/publish) ?

11 The money _____ (give) to him by his parents.

C Change the active sentences into passive sentences. Use the words in brackets.

0 We sell tickets for all shows at the Box Office.
(Tickets for all shows / sell / at the Box Office) _Tickets for all shows are sold at the Box Office._

1 Thomas Edison invented the electric light bulb
(The electric light bulb / invent / by Thomas Edison) _____

2 Someone painted the office last week.
(The office / paint / last week) _____

3 Several people saw the accident.
(The accident / see / by several people) _____

4 Where do they make these video recorders?
(Where / these video recorders / make) _____

5 Six countries signed the agreement.
(The agreement / sign / by six countries) _____

6 A stranger helped me.
(I / help / by a stranger) _____

7 They don't deliver the post on Sundays.
(The post / not / deliver / on Sundays) _____

D Put in the correct active or passive form in brackets ( ).

Fiat
Fiat ⁰ _was started_____ (started/was started) by a group of Italian businessmen in 1899. In 1903, Fiat ¹_____ (produced/was produced) 132 cars. Some of these cars ²_____ (exported/were exported) by the company to the United States and Britain. In 1920, Fiat ³_____ (started/was started) making cars at a new factory at Lingotto, near Turin. There was a track on the roof where the cars ⁴_____ (tested/were tested) by technicians. In 1936, Fiat launched the Fiat 500. This car ⁵_____ (called/was called) the Topolino – the Italian name for Mickey Mouse. The company grew, and in 1963 Fiat ⁶_____ (exported/was exported) more than 300,000 vehicles. Today, Fiat is based in Turin, and its cars ⁷_____ (sold/are sold) all over the world.

27 Verb + -ing (I like cooking); like and would like

1 Look at this example:

-ing FORM

*I **like** | listening | to music.*

(For details on **-ing** forms, see Table C on page 95.)

We can use certain verbs (e.g. **like**) with an **-ing** form:

like enjoy love keep finish stop mind	+ -ing FORM

*She doesn't **like cooking**.*
*Do you **enjoy driving**?*
*They **love living** in a village.*
*He **keeps saying** the same things.*
  (= He says the same things many times.)
*Have you **finished eating**?*
*Suddenly she **stopped talking**.*
*I don't **mind waiting**.*

2 Compare this pair of sentences:

> *I **like** working here.*
>   *(= I enjoy my job here.)*
> *I'd **like** (= I would like) to get a better job.*
>   *(= I want to get a better job.)*

We use **like** + **-ing** (e.g. **like listening**, like

working) to talk about things that we enjoy doing. We use **would like to** to say that we want to do something. Here are some more examples:

*She **likes painting** pictures.*
  (= She enjoys painting pictures.)
*She **would like to be** an artist.*
  (= She wants to be an artist.)

*I **like going** to the theatre.*
  (= I enjoy going to the theatre.)
*I'd **like to go** to the theatre tonight.*
  (= I want to go to the theatre tonight.)

*Do you **like playing** cards?*
  (= Do you enjoy playing cards?)
***Would** you **like to play** cards now?*
  (= Do you want to play now?)

In offers and requests it is more polite to say **would like** than **want**:

***Would** you **like to come** for dinner?* (offer)
*I'd **like to leave** work early, please.* (request)

3 We use **go** + **-ing** for sports and hobbies that we go out to do, and with **shopping**:

*We often **go skiing** in the winter.*
*Let's **go swimming** this afternoon.*
*She **goes dancing** at weekends.*
*I'm **going shopping** this afternoon.*

....

Practice

A Complete the sentences using a Present Simple form of the first verb in brackets. Study the example first.

0 She _likes playing_____ (like/play) tennis, but she _doesn't like watching_____ (not/like/watch) it.

1 The buses _____ (stop/run) at midnight.

2 I _____ (not/mind/listen) to his problems.

3 He's not very good at playing chess, so he _____ (keep/lose).

4 She _____ (enjoy/go) to other countries and she _____ (like/meet) new people.

5 I _____ (keep/make) the same stupid mistakes!

6 They usually _____ (finish/eat) at about 8.30 in the evening.

7 She _____ (not/enjoy/drive), but she _____ (love/cycle).

8 _____ (you/like/read) detective novels?

9 I _____ (not/mind/change) the time of our appointment.

10 Please _____ (stop/make) that terrible noise!

B **Complete the sentences using *like/not like* + *-ing* or *would like* + *to* with the words in brackets.**

  0 She <u>doesn't like working</u> (work) here. She hates this job
     and is going to look for a better one.

  0 <u>Would you like to watch</u> (you / watch) a different programme,
     or do you want to watch this one?

  1 I _____ (live) here. I have lived here for many years
     and I think it's a nice town.

  2 Sarah _____ (be) a journalist when she leaves university.
     She wants to work on a newspaper or a magazine.

  3 I _____ (get up) so early every morning, but I have to do it.

  4 I _____ (go out) for dinner in an Italian restaurant tonight.

  5 Clare _____ (find) a job in the United States. She wants
     to work in Boston or in New York.

  6 I _____ (watch) television all the time; I think it's a waste of time.

  7 Mary _____ (lie) on the beach when she's on holiday.
     She doesn't like swimming or going on trips.

  8 I _____ (discuss) something important with you this afternoon.

  9 _____ (you/come) to a party at my house next Saturday?

 10 I _____ (do) nothing this weekend — I'm very tired.

 11 Jane _____ (go) to parties; she always enjoys them.

 12 Bruce _____ (cook), so he often eats in restaurants.

 13 A: Susan is working as a secretary in an office in the centre of London.
     B: _____ (work) in an office?
     A: No, she hates it. She _____ (find) a different job.

 14 A: What _____ (you/do) next summer?
     B: I _____ (visit) South America, but I might not have enough money.

C **Look at the pictures. They show what John did last week on holiday.**
Complete the sentences using the correct form of *go* and a verb from the box.

dance
~~shop~~
sail
swim
ski
cycle

0 Monday

1 Tuesday

2 Wednesday

3 Thursday

4 Friday

5 Saturday

  0 On Monday <u>he went shopping.</u> _____
  1 On Tuesday _____
  2 On Wednesday _____
  3 On Thursday _____
  4 On Friday _____
  5 On Saturday _____

28 To + infinitive (**I want to go**) or infinitive (**I can go**)

1 Look at this example:

to + INFINITIVE

I want | **to buy** | *some stamps.*

We use **to do, to buy, to start** etc. (**to** + infinitive) after these verbs:

want	decide
agree	promise
forget	offer
hope	plan
arrange	try

} + **to** + INFINITIVE

*She **agreed to lend** him some money.*
*He **forgot to book** the tickets.*
*I'm **hoping to get** a new bike soon.*
*I've **arranged to play** tennis tonight.*
*They've **decided to start** a new company.*
*You **promised to help** me.*
*She **offered to do** the washing-up.*
*We're **planning to go** away this weekend.*
*He's **trying to learn** French.*

2 We can also say **want** + someone + **to**:
*His parents **want him to go** to university.*
*Do you **want me to help** you?*

3 Now look at this example:

INFINITIVE

*He **can*** | **speak** | *Spanish.*

Can is a modal verb. We use **do, speak, see** etc. (infinitives) after a modal verb. Some of the most common modal verbs are:

will ('ll) should may
might can could must

} + INFINITIVE

I'll see you soon.
*She **won't agree.***
*Where **should I sit?***
*We **may go** by train.*
*It **may not cost** much.*
Can I park here?
*I **couldn't hear** her.*
*We **must pay** now.*

4 We can use **make** + someone + **infinitive**, to mean 'cause' or 'force':
*The film **made me cry.***
   (= It caused me to cry.)
*They **made us leave.***
   (= They forced us to leave.)

5 We can use **let** + someone + **infinitive**, to mean 'allow':
*She **let me stay**.* (= She allowed me to stay.)

···

Practice

A Put the verbs in brackets ( ) into these sentences. Use an infinitive (*phone*) or *to* + infinitive (*to phone*).

0   You can't __smoke_____ (smoke) here. Smoking is not allowed in this building.

1   I'm sorry I forgot _____ (phone) you yesterday. I was very busy.

2   Don't worry. The exam may not _____ (be) very difficult.

3   My boss makes me _____ (work) very hard.

4   It's not a very good film. You won't _____ (enjoy) it.

5   She didn't want _____ (wait) any longer, so she left.

6   When are you planning _____ (eat) tonight?

7   She couldn't _____ (reply) because she didn't know what to say.

8   This kind of music makes me _____ (feel) good.

9   Our boss sometimes lets us _____ (leave) early.

10   I'm afraid I've forgotten _____ (bring) the map.

11   They might not _____ (receive) the letter until next week.

B Complete each sentence so that it has the same meaning as the sentence in brackets.

0 (I don't think it's a good idea to argue with him.)
   I don't think you should _argue with him._

1 (I won't be able to come to the meeting on Friday.)
   I can't _____

2 (I'm meeting some friends tonight.)
   I've arranged _____

3 (Listen to what I'm telling you.)
   I want you _____

4 (It's important that you lock the door when you go out.)
   Don't forget _____

5 (Perhaps we'll go out for a meal this evening.)
   We may _____

6 (Allow me to pay for the meal.)
   Let _____

7 (I'd like to do a course in Art History.)
   I want _____

8 (He said, 'I'll pay the bill'.)
   He offered _____

9 (Should I sit in this chair?)
   Do you want me _____?

10 (His stories were very funny, and I laughed a lot.)
   His funny stories made _____

11 (Perhaps he'll phone you tomorrow.)
   He might _____

12 (It's possible that Tom won't be angry with you.)
   Tom might not _____

13 (Jane allowed me to drive her new car.)
   Jane let _____

C Complete the conversation, using the verbs in brackets with or without *to*.

Charles: I want ⁰ _to do_____ (do) something interesting this weekend. Can we
          ¹_____ (do) something together?

Diana: Well, I've arranged ²_____ (go) on a trip to the coast with
          some friends. Do you want ³_____ (come) with us?

Charles: Yes, that sounds good. When are you planning ⁴_____ (leave) ?

Diana: Well, we've decided ⁵_____ (start) early in the morning tomorrow,
          and I've promised ⁶_____ (take) the others in my car.
          We're hoping ⁷_____ (reach) the coast by lunchtime. So, you must
          ⁸_____ (meet) me here at 6.30 a.m.

Charles: Okay, good. I won't ⁹_____ (be) late.

29 Reported speech; say/said or tell/told

1 When we report something that somebody said, we usually change the tense of the verb like this:

ACTUAL WORDS	REPORTED SPEECH
Present Simple 'I live in a small flat,' she said.	→ Past Simple She said she **lived** in a small flat.
Present Continuous 'I'm leaving on Tuesday,' I said.	→ Past Continuous I said that I **was leaving** on Tuesday.
Past Simple Present Perfect } 'I learnt a lot,' he said. 'Mr Jackson has left,' she said.	→ Past Perfect He said he **had learnt** a lot. She said that Mr Jackson **had left**.
will 'I'll help you,' she said.	→ would She said she **would help** me.
am/is/are going to 'We're going to be late,' I said.	→ was/were going to I said that we **were going** to be late.
can 'I can't find my money,' he said.	→ could He said he **couldn't** find his money.

2 Note that it is not necessary to use **that** in reported speech:

*She said (**that**) she knew the answer.*

3 Compare **say** and **tell** in these sentences:

*She **said** (that) she lived in a small flat.*
*She **told me** (that) she lived in a small flat.*

We **say something**. We do not **say someone something**.

She said she was going to be late.
 (Not ~~She said me she was ...~~)
I said that I disagreed with him.
 (Not ~~I said him that I ...~~)

We **tell someone something**. We do not **tell something**.

*He told **me** he was happy.*
 (Not ~~He told he was happy.~~)
*He told **me** that he would pay me immediately.*
 (Not ~~He told that he would pay me immediately.~~)
*She told **Fred** she was going to meet someone.*
 (Not ~~She told that she was going to meet someone.~~)

....

Practice

A Look at these pictures of people coming through passport control at an airport. Change the things they said into reported speech.

0
1
2
3
4
5

0 He said ___that he was visiting friends.___

1 She said _____

2 He said _____

3 They said _____

4 She said _____

5 They said _____

B **Read this conversation and then report what Claudia and Nicole said.**

Nicole: How long have you been in France?

Claudia: Six weeks.

Nicole: Are you enjoying your stay?

Claudia: Yes, I'm enjoying it a lot.

Nicole: Have you been here before?

Claudia: Yes. I've been to France many times.

Nicole: What are you doing here?

Claudia: I'm on holiday.

Nicole: Are you staying in a hotel?

Claudia: No, I'm staying with some friends.

Nicole: Where do they live?

Claudia: They have a flat in the city centre.

Nicole: How long are you staying?

Claudia: I'm leaving in March.

Nicole: Can you speak French very well?

Claudia: No, I can't. I'm going to have some lessons.

Nicole: I'll teach you.

0 Claudia said _that she had been_ _____ in France for six weeks.

1 Claudia said _____ her stay a lot.

2 Claudia said _____ to France many times.

3 Claudia said _____ on holiday.

4 She said _____ with some friends.

5 She said _____ a flat in the city centre.

6 She said _____ in March.

7 She said _____ French very well.

8 She said _____ some lessons.

9 Nicole said _____ Claudia.

C **Complete the sentences with *said* or *told*.**

0 She __*said*____ she wasn't feeling very well.

1 Alex _____ me that he would buy the tickets.

2 They _____ that the train was going to be late.

3 She _____ him that she was very angry with him.

4 She _____ him that she couldn't help him.

5 Who _____ you that I was leaving? It's not true!

6 They _____ us that they were leaving in the morning.

7 He _____ that he didn't know what was wrong with the car.

8 She _____ she had four sisters.

9 She _____ me that Tom worked in a factory.

10 He _____ me that he was a doctor, but he _____ Anna that
   he was a dentist.

30 Articles: **a/an**, **the**, or no article

1 We use **a/an** with singular nouns:
*He was reading **a book**.*

We use **an** before vowel sounds (**a,e,i,o,u**):
***an** apple   **an** interesting film*
***an** hour* (pronounced 'our')

2 Now look at this example:
*When I arrived, John was reading **a book**.*

We use **a/an** when it isn't necessary to make clear which particular thing we are talking about. There are lots of books; John was reading one of them.

We use **a/an** to talk about people's jobs:
*Jim is **an engineer**.* (= There are lots of engineers; Jim is one.)

We use **a/an** to describe things or people:
*They have **a beautiful house**.* (= There are lots of beautiful houses; they have one.)
*John is **an old friend** of mine.*

3 We use **the** with singular or plural nouns:
***the** book   **the** books*

We can use **the** with uncountable nouns (e.g. **music, water, food, education**):
***The water** is in the fridge.*
Note:
▶ uncountable nouns do not have a plural (not ~~2 musics~~, ~~three waters~~).
▶ we do not use **a/an** with uncountable nouns (not ~~a music~~, ~~a water~~).

4 We use **the** when it is clear which person or thing we are talking about:
*Jean was reading **a book**. She closed **the book**.* (= She closed the book that she was reading.)
*Anna likes music, but she doesn't like **the music** that John plays.*
*Mike's gone to **the shops**.* (= the local shops)
*She's in **the kitchen**.* (= the kitchen in this house)
*I must go to **the bank**.* (= my bank, where I keep my money)
the centre/the station/the airport (in a city)
the River Thames (There is only one.)
the government *in my country*

5 We do not use **the** before plural nouns (e.g. **vegetables**) or uncountable nouns (e.g. **education, music**) when we are talking about something in general:
*Do you like **vegetables**?* (= any vegetables)
*I think **education** is very important.*

6 We do not use **a** or **the** before names of languages, meal names, the names of cities, most countries and most streets, and the names of airports, stations, single mountains or lakes:
*She speaks **Spanish**.*
*She lives in **Amsterdam** in **Holland**.* (But we say **the** U.S.A., **the** United Kingdom.)
*What time will **lunch** be?*
*from **Heathrow Airport** to **Oxford Street***

. . . .

Practice

A Put *a*, *an* or *the* into the gaps if they are required. Leave the gaps empty if nothing is required.

0 I want to put some money into my bank account, so I'm going to __the__ bank this afternoon. It's in ___–___ Midland Street.

1 I had _____ sandwich for _____ lunch today.

2 We flew to _____ Dublin Airport in _____ Ireland.

3 It was _____ long flight, but eventually we arrived in _____ U.S.A.

4 I'm trying to learn _____ Japanese. I'm having _____ lesson tomorrow.

5 He made _____ angry speech against _____ government.

6 She is _____ famous actress and she is appearing in _____ popular TV series.

7 They live in _____ Paris in _____ area near to _____ River Seine.

8 They've bought _____ small flat in _____ Park Street.

B Complete the sentences by putting in *a*, *an* or *the* if required. Leave the gap empty if nothing is required. (Note that the following words in this exercise are uncountable nouns: *music, fuel, education, fish, food, coffee, exercise.*)

0 She read __the__ letters that had arrived that morning.

1 It was a nice day, so we had _____ lunch in _____ garden of my house.

2 I'm just going to _____ shops. I'll be back in a few minutes.

3 We phoned for _____ taxi to take us to _____ airport.

4 I like listening to _____ music when I come home.

5 Without _____ fuel, _____ cars don't work.

6 John was at home. He was reading _____ magazine in _____ living-room.

7 His parents believe that _____ education is a very important thing.

8 Jane doesn't like _____ fish; she never eats it.

9 After _____ dinner, I washed _____ plates and glasses.

10 Did you like _____ food at _____ party yesterday?

11 A: Where's _____ coffee?

    B: It's in _____ cupboard next to _____ sink.

12 Doctors say that _____ exercise is good for everybody.

C Complete this conversation by putting in *a*, *an* or *the* if required. Leave the gap empty if nothing is required.

Mike: Is Maria [0] __a__ student at your college?

Rosie: No, she's [1] _____ old friend of mine. We were at school together.

Mike: What does she do now?

Rosie: She's [2] _____ computer programmer. She's not English, you know. She comes from [3] _____ Brazil, but she's living in [4] _____ U.S.A. at the moment.

Mike: Has she got [5] _____ job there?

Rosie: Yes, she's working for [6] _____ big company there.

Mike: Do you write [7] _____ letters to each other?

Rosie: Yes, and I had [8] _____ long letter from her yesterday.

Mike: What did she say in [9] _____ letter?

Rosie: She said that she was living in [10] _____ nice apartment in [11] _____ centre of [12] _____ Chicago.

D Complete the story by putting *a*, *an* or *the* into the gaps.

Yesterday I was sitting on [0] __the__ 6 o'clock train when I saw [1] _____ strange man walking along the platform. He came into the carriage of [2] _____ train where I was sitting, and he sat in the seat opposite mine. He opened [3] _____ newspaper and started reading it. On [4] _____ front page of [5] _____ newspaper, there was [6] _____ picture of [7] _____ bank robber. The words under [8] _____ picture were: 'Wanted by the police'. It was [9] _____ same man!

31 Myself, yourself etc; each other

1 Look at this table:

SUBJECT PRONOUNS	OBJECT PRONOUNS	REFLEXIVE PRONOUNS
I	me	myself
you (*singular*)	you	yourself
he	him	himself
she	her	herself
it	it	itself
we	us	ourselves
you (*plural*)	you	yourselves
they	them	themselves

2 Compare:

(i)

Jenny made Jo a cup of coffee.
(= Jenny made the coffee for Jo.)

(ii)

*Jenny made **herself** a cup of coffee.*
(= Jenny made the coffee for herself.)

We use **myself**, **yourself**, **herself** etc. to refer to the subject:

SUBJECT		

Be careful. **You** might hurt **yourself**.

*I bought **myself** a new shirt.*
*He taught **himself** to swim.*
*They enjoyed **themselves** at the concert.*

3 We also use **myself**, **yourself** etc. to emphasize that the subject did the action, not another person:
*He built the whole house **himself**.*
   (= He built it alone; nobody helped him.)

4 We use **each other** like this:
*Tom and Sue were talking to **each other**.*
   (= Tom was talking to Sue, and Sue was talking to Tom.)
*We like **each other** very much.* (= I like her and she likes me.)

Compare **themselves** and **each other**:
*Alan and Ruth took these photographs **themselves**.* (= They took them, not another person.)
*Alan and Ruth took photographs of **each other**.* (= Alan took a photograph of Ruth, and Ruth took a photograph of Alan.)

••

Practice

A Fill the gaps with *myself, yourself* etc.

0 I cooked __myself__ a meal and then I watched television.

1 I'm sure he'll enjoy _____ on his trip.

2 I cut _____ while I was preparing the vegetables.

3 We amused _____ by playing cards while we were waiting for the plane.

4 She put the plates on the table and told them to help _____ to the food.

5 Tom hurt _____ when he was playing football.

6 Alan cooked _____ a snack when he got home.

B Complete the sentences with the correct verb tenses and *myself, yourself* etc. in the correct place.

0 (Be careful with that knife or you / cut /.)
   Be careful with that knife or _you'll cut yourself._

1 (It was a very nice trip and we / enjoy / very much.)
   It was a very nice trip and we _____

2 (I / burn / while I was taking the dish out of the oven.)

   I _____ while I was taking the dish out of the oven.

3 (He didn't have lessons. He / teach /.)

   He didn't have lessons. _____

4 (I think I / buy / a new coat tomorrow.)

   _____

5 (She / make / a sandwich and ate it in the kitchen.)

   _____ and ate it in the kitchen.

C Fill the gaps with *myself, yourself* etc.

0 Did you paint the room _yourself_ ? ~ Yes, it took me three days to do it.

1 If you won't help me, I'll have to do it all _____ .

2 She makes all her clothes _____ .

3 The students organized the concert _____ .

4 We painted the whole house _____ .

5 He typed the letter _____ and then he posted it.

D Complete the sentences with the correct verb tenses and *myself, yourself* etc. Put *myself, yourself* etc. at the end of the sentence.

0 (She is a very successful singer. She / write / all her songs /.)

   She is a very successful singer. _She writes all her songs herself._

1 Could you post this letter for me? ~ (No, I'm sorry, I won't have time. You / have / to post it /.)

   No, I'm sorry, I won't have time. _____

2 (Nobody helped us, so we / carry / all our luggage /.)

   Nobody helped us, so _____

3 (This is an excellent photograph. / you / take it /?)

   This is an excellent photograph. _____

4 (She was wearing a dress that she / make /.)

   She was wearing a dress that _____

5 (I hope you like the present. I / choose / it /.)

   I hope you like the present. _____

6 (Do you like this meal? I / invent / the recipe /.)

   Do you like this meal? _____

E Fill the gaps with *each other, ourselves, yourselves* or *themselves*.

0 They spent the whole evening arguing with _each other_ .

0 Their house is very beautiful; they designed it _themselves_ .

1 Mary met John in April, but they didn't see _____ again until July.

2 They're not friends; in fact, they don't like _____ at all.

3 Don't ask me to help you. You must do it _____ .

4 We didn't buy it _____ . A friend bought it for us.

5 I could hear two people shouting at _____ .

6 We're working in the same office now, so Ron and I see _____ every day.

32 Direct and indirect objects (**She gave him a book**)

1 Look at this example:

Thank you.

(i) She gave **her brother** the newspaper.
(ii) She gave the newspaper **to her brother**.
In both sentences **a newspaper** is the thing which is given, and **her brother** is the person who receives it.

2 Here are other sentences like (i) *She gave **her brother** the newspaper*:

	+ PERSON (indirect object)	+ THING (direct object)
She **gave**	her brother	a shirt.
He **sent**	me	a letter.
I **showed**	him	my passport.
Jane **lent**	Frank	some money.
I'll **offer**	her	a job.
I'll **cook**	them	a meal.
I **fetched**	her	a plate.
I'll **get**	you	a magazine.
I'll **buy**	you	a coffee.

3 Here are some other sentences like (ii) *She gave the newspaper **to her brother***:

	+ THING (direct object)	+ PERSON (**to** + object)
She **gave**	a shirt	**to** her brother.
I **sent**	postcards	**to** my friends.
I **showed**	my card	**to** the clerk.
She **lent**	some money	**to** her friend.
He **offered**	the chocolates	**to** the others.

Note that we use **to** + object after these verbs which express the idea of giving or showing something to somebody:
give, send, show, lend, offer

But we use **for** + object after verbs which express the idea of doing something for another person:
cook, fetch, buy, get (= 'fetch' or 'buy')

	+ THING (direct object)	+ PERSON (**for** + object)
We **cooked**	a meal	**for** everybody.
He **fetched**	the newspaper	**for** his father.
I'll **get**	your book	**for** you.
She **bought**	some toys	**for** them.

....

Practice

A **Put these words into the right order to make sentences. Do not add any words.**

0 (He – lent – his car – Mark)
   He lent Mark his car.

1 (a cigarette – Jim – She offered)
   _____

2 (Mary – his holiday photographs – He showed)
   _____

3 (them – an invitation – Have you sent – ?)
   _____

4 (a birthday present – Did you buy – her – ?)
   _____

5 (I – some of my tapes – a friend – gave)
   _____

6 (When you go to the post office, – some stamps – me – could you get – ?)
   _____

B Now write the sentences from Exercise A again, but using *to* or *for*.

0 He lent _his car to Mark._

1 She offered _____

2 He showed _____

3 Have you sent _____

4 Did you buy _____

5 I gave _____

6 When you go to the post office, could you get _____

C Change these sentences. In each case use the other possible structure.

0 He offered his seat to an old lady.
   He offered an old lady his seat.

1 I have sent Jane a birthday card.

   _____

2 I don't want to lend my bike to Bruce.

   _____

3 I gave your message to Joan.

   _____

4 Could you fetch me a knife and fork?

   _____

D Tim and Lucy went to a restaurant last night for a meal. Make sentences
   about what happened while they were there. Write two sentences. Use the
   words in brackets ( ).

0 (The waiter / give / the menu.)
   (her) _The waiter gave her the menu._
   (to Lucy) _The waiter gave the menu to Lucy._

1 (The waiter / fetch / some wine.)
   (them) _____
   (for them) _____

2 (The waiter / show / the bottle.)
   (him) _____
   (to Tim) _____

3 (The chef / cook / a special meal.)
   (them) _____
   (for them) _____

4 (The waiter / give / the bill.)
   (Tim) _____
   (to Tim) _____

5 (Lucy / lend / some money, because he didn't have enough to pay the bill.)
   (Tim) _____
   (to Tim) _____

33 something, anybody, nothing etc.

1 **something** / **anything** = a thing
somebody / **anybody** = a person
someone / **anyone** = a person
somewhere / **anywhere** = a place

2 We usually use **something**, **somebody**, **someone** and **somewhere** in positive sentences:
Something is burning. (= I can smell burning. I don't know what is burning.)
*I'm going to have **something** to eat.*
(= I'm going to eat; I don't know what I'm going to eat.)
Somebody told me that it was a good film.
(= A person told me it was a good film. I can't remember who told me.)
*She lives **somewhere** in the north.*

3 We usually use **anything**, **anybody**, **anyone** and **anywhere** in negative sentences, and in questions:
*I didn't know **anyone** at the party.*
(= There were no people at the party who I knew.)
*I couldn't find my bag **anywhere**.*
(= I couldn't find my bag in any place.)
*Did you understand **anything** she said?*

4 **nothing** = not anything
nobody = not anybody
no one = not anyone
nowhere = not anywhere

We use **nothing**, **nobody**, **no one** and **nowhere** before or after positive verbs:
Nothing makes Joe unhappy. (= There isn't anything that makes Joe unhappy.)
*There's **nothing** I want to watch on TV.*
Nobody was there when I arrived.
*There **is nowhere** that I would prefer to live than here.* (= There isn't anywhere . . .)

5 We can use **else** after **something**, **anybody**, **nowhere** etc:
*Let's talk about **something else**.*
(= Let's talk about a different subject.)
*I didn't tell **anybody else**.*
(= I didn't tell another person.)
*There is **nowhere else** I can look for it.*

6 We can also use an adjective (e.g. **wrong**, **nice**) after **something**, **anything** etc:
*Have I said **something wrong**?*

....

Practice

A **Put in the correct word from the box in each gap.**

> anything (×2)   nobody (×2)   ~~somebody~~   somewhere (×2)
> nothing (×3)   something   anywhere

0 _Somebody_____ phoned you today, but he didn't tell me his name.

1 Everybody was having lunch in the restaurant, so there was _____ in the office.

2 She didn't say _____ about her job when I spoke to her.

3 I'm sure you'll find it _____ if you keep looking.

4 I had to go to the cinema on my own because _____ wanted to go with me.

5 A: Are you worried about something?
   B: No, _____ is worrying me.

6 Can I speak to you for a moment? I want to discuss _____ with you.

7 Unfortunately, I couldn't help. There was _____ I could do about the problem.

8 A: What did you buy at the shops?
   B: I bought _____. I couldn't find _____ that I liked.

9 A: Have you seen my handbag _____?
   B: Yes, I think it's _____ in the living-room.

B Choose the correct verb form in brackets.

0 I'm afraid I _don't know_____ (know/don't know) anything about this subject.

0 I rang the doorbell but nobody _was_____ (was/wasn't) in.

1 I asked a lot of people, but nobody _____ (knew/didn't know) the answer.

2 I _____ (have seen/haven't seen) anything so lovely before in my life!

3 I _____ (ate/didn't eat) anything for lunch yesterday.

4 Nothing interesting _____ (has happened/hasn't happened) since the last time I spoke to you.

5 He loves football. Nothing else _____ (is/isn't) important to him.

6 She _____ (said/didn't say) anything about her plans for the future.

C Change each of these sentences into a sentence with the same meaning. Use the word in brackets with the **underlined** adjective or with *else.*

0 A **strange** thing happened yesterday. (something)
   _Something strange_____ happened yesterday.

0 Let's listen to some different music. (something)
   Let's listen to _something else_____.

1 Is there an **interesting** programme on TV tonight? (anything)
   Is there _____ on TV tonight?

2 You won't find better food in any other place. (anywhere)
   You won't find better food _____.

3 Is there a **cheap** place we can go for lunch? (anywhere)
   Is there _____ we can go for lunch?

4 Let's sit in a different place. (somewhere)
   Let's sit _____.

5 I'd like a **hot** drink. (something)
   I'd like _____ to drink.

D Put the right form of a word beginning with *some-*, *any-* or *no-* into the conversation.

Dennis: Have you read ⁰ _anything_____ interesting lately?

Sarah: Yes, ¹ _____ lent me a novel last week and I really enjoyed it.

Dennis: What was it about?

Sarah: It was about ² _____ who goes to visit Australia. A few days after she arrives there, ³ _____ terrible happens to her.

Dennis: What?

Sarah: While she is travelling across Australia, she loses her passport and all her money. She doesn't know ⁴ _____ who can help her, and she hasn't got ⁵ _____ to stay.

Dennis: What happens then?

Sarah: I'm not going to tell you ⁶ _____ else! You should read the book yourself.

Dennis: It sounds like a very depressing book! I don't think I'll read it.

Sarah: You would like it. ⁷ _____ wonderful happens at the end.

34 All, most, some, none

1 We use

> **all/most/some** + NOUN   (e.g. **most cities**)

to talk about things or people in general:
> *She thinks that **all sports** are boring.*
>   (= She thinks that **every sport** is boring.)
> ***Most cities** have a lot of shops.*
>   (= **Almost every city** has a lot of shops.)
> *In **some countries** life is very hard.*
>   (= In a number of countries in the world,
>   but not **all** or **most** …)

We do not say **all/most/some** + of + noun:
> ***Most people** take exams during their lives.*
>   (Not ~~*Most of people* …~~)

2 We can also use **all** with **morning/
afternoon/evening/night/day/week/year**
(e.g. **all afternoon**) to mean 'the whole',
'from the beginning to the end of':

*They've been working hard **all day**.*

*I waited for the phone call **all morning**.*

3 We use

> **all/most**
> **some/none** $\Big\}$ + of + the/my/her + NOUN
> (e.g. **all of my books**)

to talk about particular things or people:
> *He spent **all of his money**.*
> *Most of **my friends** are interested in sport.*
> *I knew **some of the people** at the party.*
> ***None of the shops** were open.*

Notice that we use a positive verb with **none**.

We can leave out **of** after **all** (but not after
most, some, none):
> *He spent **all his money**.*

4 We can use

> **all/most/some/none** + of + it/them

when we have already mentioned the noun
that **it** or **them** refers to:
> *It was lovely food, but I couldn't eat **all of it**.*
>   (**it** = the food)
> *I phoned a number of hotels, but **most of
>   them** were full.* (**them** = the hotels)
> *That cake looks nice. Can I have **some of it**?*
>   (**it** = the cake)

....

Practice

A   Look at these exam results for four people and complete the sentences,
using *all of*, *some of*, *most of* or *none of*. Sometimes you will need *the*
(e.g. *some of the*).

Student	Exam 1	Exam 2	Exam 3	Exam 4	Exam 5	Exam 6
Alice	PASS	PASS	FAIL	PASS	PASS	PASS
Bill	PASS	PASS	PASS	PASS	PASS	PASS
Carol	FAIL	PASS	PASS	PASS	FAIL	FAIL
David	FAIL	FAIL	FAIL	FAIL	FAIL	FAIL

0   Alice passed _*most of the*_ exams.

1   Bill passed _____ exams.

2   Bill failed _____ them.

3   Carol passed _____ exams.

4   Carol passed _____ them.

5   Carol failed _____ them.

6   David passed _____ them.

7   David passed _____ exams.

8   David failed _____ exams.

B Complete the sentences by putting in the correct words from the box.

| all   some   all the   some of the   none of the |

0 _All_____ children have to go to school in this country by law.

0 The classroom was empty because _all the_____ children had gone home.

1 We couldn't buy anything because _____ shops in the area were closed.

2 A: Where were you at 3 o'clock yesterday afternoon?

   B: I was at home. I was at home _____ afternoon. I didn't go out
      until the evening.

3 We went to a restaurant last night. _____ food was lovely, but I didn't
   like the soup or the dessert.

4 _____ people say that he's the best tennis player in the world, but
   a lot of others don't agree.

5 It was a very boring day. _____ places that we visited were interesting.

6 He spent _____ morning reading the newspaper, so he didn't do any work.

7 _____ phones in the station worked, so I couldn't phone you.

8 We left the hotel at 9 o'clock in the morning, and we didn't go back to the hotel until the
   evening. We walked round the city, looking at the sights, _____ day.

9 _____ jackets fitted me, so I didn't buy one.

10 _____ passengers must buy a ticket before they travel.

11 She was ill. She stayed in bed from Monday to Saturday. She didn't go to work
    _____ week.

12 The teacher asked a question, but _____ students knew the answer, so the teacher
    told them.

13 _____ course was difficult for me, but most of it was easy.

C Complete the sentences by putting in the correct words from the box.

all of	all of it	most of them
most of	all of them	none of it
none of	most of it	none of them

0 I watched _most of_____ the programme, but I didn't watch _all of it_____.

1 I've read _____ the book, but I haven't read _____ yet. I'm
   reading the last chapter.

2 She did _____ the decorating herself, but she didn't do _____.
   A friend helped her with some of it.

3 A: Did you understand _____ the words in that story?

   B: No, but I understood _____. There were only a few that I didn't know.

4 I rang _____ the hotels in the town, but _____ had
   vacant rooms, so we had nowhere to stay.

5 _____ the pens on my desk work; _____ are empty. Can I
   borrow yours?

6 I did _____ the work that I had to do. I finished at midnight. It took me a very
   long time to do it, because _____ was easy.

35 Both (. . . and), either (. . . or), neither (. . . nor)

1 We use **both**, **either** and **neither** to talk about two things or people. Look at this example with **both ...and**:

*Both the white jumper **and** the black jumper are nice. He doesn't know which one to buy.*

We can also say:
Both jumpers are nice.

2 Now look at this example with **either ... or**:

*Jeff would like to visit **either** Australia **or** India, but he can't decide which one.*

We can also say:
*Jeff **would like** to visit **either country**.*

We can also use a negative verb with **either**:
*Jeff **hasn't been** to **either** country.*

3 Now look at this example:

*Neither the black jacket **nor** the white jacket fitted her.*

Or we can say:
Neither jacket fitted her.

Note that we do not use a negative verb with **neither**:

Not ~~Neither jacket didn't fit her.~~

~~Jeff hasn't been to neither country.~~

4 We can also use **both**, **either**, and **neither** like this:

both either neither	of	the my his these	PLURAL NOUN

PLURAL VERB
Both of these suitcases **are** *heavy.*

*I haven't seen **either of the films**.*

SINGULAR or PLURAL VERB
Neither of his sisters **was/were** *there.*

We can also say:

both/either/neither + of + them/us

*He has two cars, but **neither of them** works.*

....

Practice

A **Fill the gaps with *either* or *neither*.**

0 I'm going to buy <u>either</u> the green shirt or the blue shirt.

1 She lent me two books, but I haven't read _____ of them.

2 John looked at Jim, but they didn't speak. _____ of them said anything.

3 _____ of the two jobs seemed very attractive, so I didn't apply for _____ of them.

4 You can have _____ fish or chicken for dinner.

5 There were two films on TV, but _____ of them looked very interesting.

6 I haven't seen _____ James or Julie this week, and _____ of them has phoned me.

7 I looked for my bag in the living-room and in the kitchen, but it wasn't in _____ room.

8 I rang two friends, but _____ of them was at home. They had gone out.

9 You can catch _____ the number 12 bus or the number 15 bus to the city centre.

10 She didn't get _____ she applied for. *[Not P.36 / first]*

11 I asked two people, b_____ f them could give me directions.

12 We can see the film _____ ht or tomorrow night.

B Look at this information _____ s. Then complete the sentences about them using *both of* _____ *of them*.

	...d Hotel	Landmark Hotel
It has a swimming pool.		✓
It is in the city centre.		✓
I t costs more than £100 a ...		✗
It offers lower prices at we...		✓
It organizes tours of the cit...		✗
It accepts credit cards.		✓
It meets guests at the airpo...		✗

0 __Both of them_____ have swimming pools.

1 _____ are in the city centre.

2 _____ costs more than £100 a night.

3 _____ offer lower prices at weekends.

4 _____ organizes tours of the city.

5 _____ accept credit cards.

6 _____ meets guests at the airport.

C Complete the sentences using *both/either/neither* + *of* + *us/them* (e.g. *neither of us*).

0 I went to the concert with Mary, but __neither of us__ enjoyed it very much because it was very boring.

1 There are two flights we can catch to New York. Both flights cost the same amount, so we can choose _____ .

2 I played two games against Harry, and I lost _____ because he is a much better player than me.

3 I saw Jane and Alison walking down the street and I waved at them, but _____ saw me because they were talking.

4 I looked at George, and George looked at me. Then _____ started to laugh because it was such a funny situation.

5 A man spoke to us but _____ could understand him, so we didn't answer.

6 Tim and I wanted to go to the game, but _____ could get tickets, so we watched it on TV.

7 I wanted to buy a new camera. There were two cameras in the shop that I liked, but they were very expensive. I couldn't afford _____ , so I didn't buy anything.

8 Ann and I worked very hard all day. _____ were very tired in the evening, so we didn't go out.

9 We went into two restaurants, but _____ were full. We couldn't get a table at either.

36 Comparative and superlative adjectives (**cheaper**, **cheapest**)

1 We use comparatives (e.g. **cheaper than**) to say that two or more things or people are different in some way:

✈	**Flights**
	Geneva £300
	Zurich £250

*The flight to Zurich is **cheaper than** the flight to Geneva.*
*The flight to Geneva is **more expensive than** the flight to Zurich.*

*It's **warmer** today **than** it was yesterday.*
*Is New York **bigger than** London?*

2 We use superlatives (e.g. **the cheapest**) like this:

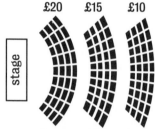

£20 £15 £10

stage

front middle back

*The **most expensive** seats are at the front of the theatre.*
*The **cheapest** seats are at the back.*

*He is **the worst** player in the team.*
*It was **the happiest** day of their lives.*

We can use a superlative without a noun:
*The seats at the back are **the cheapest**.*

3 Look at these tables:

▶ short adjectives (1 syllable):

warm	warm**er**	the warm**est**
tall	tall**er**	the tall**est**
low	low**er**	the low**est**
big	big**ger**	the big**gest**
hot	hot**ter**	the hot**test**
wet	wet**ter**	the wet**test**

▶ long adjectives (2 syllables or more):

famous	**more** famous	the **most** famous
beautiful	**more** beautiful	the **most** beautiful

▶ adjectives ending with -**y**:

easy	eas**ier**	the eas**iest**
happy	happ**ier**	the happ**iest**

▶ irregular adjectives:

good	**better**	the **best**
bad	**worse**	the **worst**

(For more details see Table F on page 97.)

4 The opposite of **more** is **less**:
*The big book is **more expensive** than the little one.*
*The little book is **less expensive** than the big one.*

....

Practice

A Look at the information about Alison and Bernard, and complete the sentences using the comparative form of the adjective in brackets ( ) and **than**.

	Alison	**Bernard**
Height:	1.6m	1.75m
Age:	30	26
Income:	£15,000 per year	£70,000 per year
Family:	2 brothers and 2 sisters	1 brother
House:	small	very big

0 Alison is <u>shorter than</u> (short) Bernard.
1 Bernard is _____ (tall) Alison.
2 Alison is _____ (old) Bernard.
3 Bernard is _____ (rich) Alison.
4 Alison's income is _____ (low) Bernard's.
5 Alison's family is _____ (big) Bernard's.
6 Alison's house is _____ (small) Bernard's.

B Complete the sentences using the comparative form of the adjective in brackets and *than*.

0 I think that golf is __more interesting than__ (interesting) tennis.
1 This question is _____ (easy) the last one.
2 I'm a good player, but Eric is _____ (good) me.
3 The group's first record was _____ (successful) their second record.
4 We both played well, but he was _____ (lucky) me.
5 Your car is _____ (powerful) mine.
6 This computer is _____ (useful) that one.

C Complete the sentences using the superlative form of the adjective in brackets.

0 Anna is __the youngest__ (young) person in her class.
1 We stayed in _____ (bad) hotel in the whole city.
2 People say that it is _____ (funny) film of the year.
3 What is _____ (tall) building in the world?
4 Her teachers say that she is _____ (good) student in the school.
5 This is _____ (expensive) camera in the shop.
6 Many people say that Venice is _____ (beautiful) city in the world.

D Complete the dialogues using the comparative form of the adjective in brackets + *than,* or the superlative form of the adjective in brackets.

0 A: Why did you choose that hotel? It's a long way from the centre of town.
   B: I chose it because it was __cheaper than__ (cheap) the hotel in the centre.
0 A: Shall we sit in the living-room?
   B: Yes, it's __the warmest__ (warm) room in the house.
1 A: Did you enjoy being a student?
   B: Yes, it was _____ (happy) period of my life.
2 A: Is he famous in this country?
   B: Yes, he's _____ (famous) any other singer.
3 A: I'm not a very good cook.
   B: I'm sure I'm _____ (bad) you. I can't cook anything well.
4 A: Do you like this programme?
   B: Yes, I think it's _____ (good) programme on TV.
5 A: What did you have for dinner?
   B: I chose _____ (expensive) dish on the menu.
6 A: How is your new course going?
   B: It's _____ (difficult) the last one I took.
7 A: What's the weather going to be like today?
   B: They say that today is going to be _____ (wet) yesterday.
8 A: Are you happy in your new flat?
   B: Yes, it's _____ (comfortable) my last one.
9 A: Is London _____ (exciting) city in Britain?
   B: No, I think that Liverpool is _____ (exciting) London.

37 Comparison: as . . . as (as strong as)

1 We use **as** + adjective + **as** (e.g. **as old as**) to say that two things or people are the same in some way:

*The chair is **as expensive as** the table.*

*You're **as old as** me.* (= We are the same age.)

Note that we say **as me / as him / as her / as us / as them**, and not **as I / as he / as she** etc:
*She's as strong as **him**.* (Not ~~. . . as he.~~)
*I'm as fast as **them**.* (Not ~~. . . as they.~~)

We use **not as . . . as** to talk about a difference between two things or people:

*The two star hotel is**n't as big as** the four star hotel.*

*I'm **not as clever as** her.* (= She is cleverer than me.)

2 We can also use **as** + adverb + **as** (e.g. **as well as**):
*Jean cooks **as well as** Tom.* (= Jean and Tom are both good cooks.)
*He couldn't run **as quickly as** Maria.* (= Maria ran more quickly than him.)

3 We use **as many** + plural noun + **as** (e.g. **as many friends as**) to say that the number of two things are equal:
*Jane has got **as many friends as** Mary.*

We use **not as many . . . as** to say two things are not equal:
*I don't have **as many books as** you.*

4 We use **as much** + uncountable noun + **as** (e.g. **as much money as**) to compare two things. Uncountable nouns are words for things that we cannot count, and so they do not have a plural form (e.g. **money**, **work**, **luggage**, **traffic**):
*Helen earns **as much money as** Colin.*
*Jack doesn't do **as much work as** me.*
*They aren't carrying **as much luggage as** us.*

Practice

A Complete each sentence so that it means the same as the one above it. Use *as* + adjective/adverb + *as*.

0 Sweden is bigger than Britain.
  Britain isn't <u>as big as Sweden</u> .

1 The other students learn more quickly than me.
  I don't learn _____ the other students.

2 You're very angry and I'm very angry also.
  I'm _____ you.

3 The seats at the front are more expensive than the seats at the back.
  The seats at the back aren't _____ the seats at the front.

4 Central Park in New York is bigger than Hyde Park in London.
  Hyde Park in London isn't _____ Central Park in New York.

5 Her last film was very good and her new film is also very good.
  Her new film is _____ her last film.

6 The other students work harder than him.
  He doesn't work _____ the other students.

B Complete the sentences about each picture, using *as . . . as* and a word from the box. Use each word once.

long	clean	fast	fresh	tall
big	~~cheap~~	strong	wide	full

0 The carrots aren't as cheap as _____ the cabbages.

1 The black car is going _____ the white car.

2 The footballers aren't _____ the basketball players.

3 Janet's hair is _____ Kathy's hair.

4 The car on the left isn't _____ the car on the right.

5 The flowers on the right aren't _____ the flowers on the left.

6 The big glass isn't _____ the little glass.

7 Jane is _____ Matthew.

8 High Street isn't _____ Main Street.

9 The black book is _____ the white book.

C Join each pair of sentences in brackets ( ), using *as much … as* or *as many … as.*

0 (I've got about 50 books. Jack's got about 100.)
I haven't got as many books as _____ Jack.

0 (You've done a lot of work. I've done a lot of work also.)
I've done as much work as _____ you.

1 (Alan earns a lot of money. Sheila only earns a little.)
Sheila doesn't earn _____ Alan.

2 (George has been to five countries. I've also been to five countries.)
I've been to _____ George.

3 (You've had five jobs. I've only had two.)
I haven't had _____ you.

4 (Tom has a lot of luggage. Jane has a lot of luggage too.)
Jane has _____ Tom.

5 (Mary answered most of the questions. I only answered about half.)
I didn't answer _____ Mary.

6 (Ruth spent £50. I also spent £50.)
I spent _____ Ruth.

38 Too and enough (too big, big enough)

1 Look at this example:

*The case is **too big**. He can't carry it.*
We use **too** to mean 'more than is good or suitable in the situation'.

2 We can use **too** like this:

> **too** + ADJECTIVE:
> *I don't want to go out. I'm **too tired**.*

> **too many** + PLURAL NOUN:
> *I couldn't find her at the concert because there were **too many people** there.*

> **too much** + UNCOUNTABLE NOUN:
> (e.g. **too much work/money/food/noise/ salt/information/time/bread**)
> *Our teacher gives us **too much work**.*

3 We can use **too** with **to** + infinitive to explain why someone cannot do something:
> *She's **too young to drive**. (= She can't drive because she's too young.)*

4 Now look at this example:

*This case is **big enough**. I can put all my clothes into it. The small case isn't **big enough**.*
We use **enough** to mean 'as much or as many as we need'. We use **not … enough** to mean 'less than we need'.

5 We can use **enough** like this:

> ADJECTIVE + **enough**:
> *Is your room **warm enough**?*

> **enough** + PLURAL NOUN:
> *I've got **enough potatoes**, thanks.*

> **enough** + UNCOUNTABLE NOUN:
> *I can't talk to you now. I haven't got **enough time**.*

6 We can also use **not … enough** + **to** + infinitive to say why someone cannot do something:
> *She isn't **old enough to drive**. (= She can't drive because she isn't old enough.)*

···

Practice

A Complete the sentences using *too* or *enough* and the word in brackets ( ).

0   I can't eat this soup because it's _too hot_____ (hot).

0   We couldn't buy the tickets because we didn't have _enough money_____ (money).

0   We didn't buy the car because it wasn't _big enough_____ (big).

1   I couldn't see her because it was _____ (dark).

2   I can't decide what to do because I haven't got _____ (information).

3   You can't change the situation now. It's _____ (late).

4   Have you had _____ (food), or would you like some more?

5   He did badly in the exam because he was _____ (nervous).

6   Slow down! You're driving _____ (fast).

7   He shouldn't play in the team because he isn't _____ (good).

8   I haven't got _____ (clothes). I must buy some more.

9   Robert didn't go to work because he didn't feel _____ (well).

10   I couldn't lift the suitcase because I wasn't _____ (strong).

11   We didn't go swimming because the water was _____ (cold).

12   Mary couldn't post all the letters because she didn't have _____ (stamps).

B Complete the sentences using *too much, too many* or *enough* and the word in brackets.

0 I'm not enjoying my job at the moment because they're giving me
   <u>too much work</u> (work).

0 Is your coffee <u>sweet enough</u> (sweet)?

1 Shall we have another coffee? Have we got _____ (time)?

2 I couldn't finish the exam because there were _____ (questions).

3 We didn't go for a walk because it wasn't _____ (warm).

4 I couldn't eat the meal because there was _____ (salt) in it.

5 Mary passed the test because she answered _____ (questions)
   correctly.

6 I didn't enjoy the party because there were _____ (people) there.

7 Is that chair _____ (comfortable) or would you like to sit here?

8 George couldn't work because the others were making _____ (noise).

9 We can't play that game because we haven't got _____ (players).

10 Shall I make some sandwiches? Have we got _____ (bread)?

11 Her work isn't very good. She makes _____ (mistakes).

C Join each pair of sentences using *too* or *enough* with *to* + infinitive (e.g. *to do, to go*).

0 Clare couldn't sleep. She was too worried.
   <u>Clare was too worried to sleep.</u>

0 I can't go on holiday. I haven't got enough money.
   <u>I haven't got enough money to go on holiday.</u>

1 I can't do any more work. I'm too tired.
   _____

2 Judy won't pass the exam. She isn't good enough.
   _____

3 Clive can't play basketball. He's too short.
   _____

4 His girl-friend couldn't go to the party. She was too ill.
   _____

5 David couldn't pay the bill. He didn't have enough money.
   _____

6 Shall we go to the beach? Is it hot enough?
   _____

7 I can't see you tonight. I'm too busy.
   _____

8 I don't want to go home. It's too early.
   _____

9 Chris couldn't repair the car. He didn't have enough tools.
   _____

10 I didn't visit all the museums. I didn't have enough time.
   _____

39 Adjectives: -ed or -ing (frightened or frightening)

1 Compare **frightened** and **frightening**:

We can use adjectives that end with **-ed** to describe people's feelings:

frightened

> SUBJECT
> *Ann* *was very **frightened**.*

The subject of the sentence (e.g. **Ann**) is the person who has the feeling.

We use an adjective that ends with **-ing** (e.g. **frightening**) to talk about a thing or person that makes us have a feeling:

frightening

> SUBJECT
> *The ghost* *was very **frightening**.*

The subject of the sentence (e.g. **the ghost**) causes the feeling.

2 Here are some more examples to compare:

*We are all **surprised** by the news.*
  (= We feel surprised.)
*I was very **tired** at the end of the journey.*
  (= I felt tired.)
*He was **excited** by the way the game ended.*
*I'm **interested** in your idea.*
*The students were **bored** during the lesson.*
*Were you **disappointed** by the film?*
*I wasn't nervous before the exam; I was **relaxed**.*

*The news is **surprising**.*
  (= The news makes us feel surprised.)
*The journey was very **tiring**.*
  (= The journey made us feel tired.)
*The end of the game was **exciting**.*
*Your idea is **interesting**.*
*The lesson was **boring**.*
*Was the film **disappointing**?*
*I went for a **relaxing** walk.*

Note that we can say:
  *The **journey** was very **tiring**.*
  or:
  *It was a very **tiring journey**.*

···

Practice

A **Choose the correct adjective in brackets ( ) to put in the gaps.**

0 It was a terrible play and I was _bored_____ (bored/boring) from start to finish.

1 I'm very _____ (excited/exciting) because I'm going to New York tomorrow.

2 Are you _____ (surprised/surprising) or were you expecting this news?

3 I'm reading a very _____ (interested/interesting) book at the moment.

4 I've had a very _____ (tired/tiring) day at work today and I want to go to bed.

5 Most people were _____ (surprised/surprising) that he won the championship.

6 I'm _____ (bored/boring). Let's go out for a cup of coffee somewhere.

7 Visit our _____ (excited/exciting) new shop!

8 His speech was very long and very _____ (bored/boring).

B Complete each sentence using the correct word from the box. Use each word once.

bored	interested	surprising	amusing	confused
boring	amused	confusing	surprised	~~interesting~~

0 Your idea is very __interesting__ . Tell me more about it.

1 He told me a very _____ story. I laughed and laughed.

2 This is a terribly _____ book. Nothing happens in it.

3 She's _____ in politics and often talks about it.

4 The map was _____ and I got lost.

5 She was _____ because she had nothing to do all day.

6 Everyone else thought it was funny, but she wasn't _____ .

7 Could you repeat that, please? I'm a bit _____ because it was very complicated.

8 It is _____ that she failed the exam, because she's a good student.

9 Everyone was _____ by the sudden noise.

C Complete the replies in these dialogues, using the correct word from the box.

confused	boring (x2)	surprised	disappointed
bored	disappointing (x2)	~~confusing~~	surprising

0 A: Do you understand what's happening in this film?
   B: No, it's very __confusing__ .

1 A: Did you think the film was good?
   B: No, I was _____ from the beginning to the end. I nearly fell asleep.

2 A: Was your trip to London as good as you expected?
   B: No, it was rather _____ . I didn't like the place. People had told
      me that London was beautiful, but I thought it was dirty and ugly.

3 A: Did you enjoy your course?
   B: No, I was _____ because I thought I would learn more.

4 A: Do you enjoy your job?
   B: No, it's very _____ . I do the same things every day.

5 A: Did you know that he was going to leave his job?
   B: No, I was very _____ . I had no idea he was planning to do that.

6 A: Do you understand the rules of this game now?
   B: No, I'm completely _____ .

7 A: Were you expecting him to get so angry?
   B: No, it was very _____ . He's usually very calm about everything.

8 A: I'm sorry to hear that you failed the exam.
   B: Yes, it was very _____ . I really wanted to pass.

9 A: Do you like watching golf on TV?
   B: No, I think it's very _____ . Nothing happens for long periods of time.

40 Adverbs (**slowly, fast**); comparative adverbs (**more quickly**)

1 Compare adverbs and adjectives:

> ADVERBS
> We use adverbs (e.g. **beautifully**) to describe how someone or something does an action:
> *Peter **plays** the violin **beautifully**.*
> (**Beautifully** describes how Peter plays.)

> ADJECTIVES
> We use adjectives (e.g. **beautiful**) to describe people or things. We use adjectives before nouns, or after **be/seem/get**:
> *Look at that **beautiful violin**!*
> *That violin **is beautiful**.*

2 We form most regular adverbs by adding -**ly** to the adjective:

> **slow → slowly   bad → badly**

> *The whole team played very **badly**.*
> *She answered all the questions **correctly**.*

If an adjective ends with -**y**, the adverb ends with -**ily**:

> **happy → happily   easy → easily**

> *We solved the problem **easily**.*

If an adjective ends with -**ble**, the adverb ends in -**bly**:

> **comfortable → comfortably**

3 Some adverbs are irregular; they do not end with -**ly**:

> **good → well**

> *He's a **good** guitar player.* (**good** = adjective)
> *He plays the guitar **well**.* (**well** = adverb)

Fast and **hard** are both adjectives and adverbs:

> **fast → fast   hard → hard**

> *Maria is a **fast** learner.* (**fast** = adjective)
> *Maria learns **fast**.* (**fast** = adverb)
> *James is a **hard** worker.* (**hard** = adjective)
> *James works **hard**.* (**hard** = adverb)

4 We form the comparative of regular adverbs with **more**:

> **carefully → more carefully**

> *You should do your work **more carefully**.*

The comparative of **well** is **better**:
> *She speaks Arabic **better** than me.*

The comparatives of **fast** and **hard** are **faster** and **harder**:
> *Could you walk **faster**? We're in a hurry.*
> *You will have to work **harder** in future.*

....

Practice

A **Put in the adjective or the adverbs in brackets ( ).**

0 The train was very ___slow_____ (slow/slowly) and I arrived late.

1 The journey took a long time because the train went very _____ (slow/slowly).

2 Mrs Green went _____ (quick/quickly) back to her office.

3 I'm afraid I can't give you an _____ (immediate/immediately) answer; I need to think about it first.

4 The work that the builders did for us was very _____ (bad/badly).

5 The builders did the work for us very _____ (bad/badly).

6 She organized the party very _____ (good/well), and everybody enjoyed it.

7 Everybody said that the party was very _____ (good/well).

8 She wrote a _____ (polite/politely) letter asking the company to give her the money back.

9 She wrote to the company and asked them _____ (polite/politely) to give her the money back.

B Complete the sentences. Put in the adverb form of the adjective in brackets ( ).

0 She read the message __quickly__ (quick).

1 Read the instructions _____ (careful).

2 He looked at her _____ (angry), but he didn't say anything.

3 She passed all her exams _____ (easy).

4 I ran as _____ (fast) as I could.

5 He thinks that he did the test _____ (bad) and that he'll fail.

6 I've been studying very _____ (hard) recently.

7 She was working _____ (busy) when I arrived.

8 She sang the song _____ (beautiful).

9 He was playing _____ (happy) when I came into the room.

10 He was concentrating _____ (hard) on his work.

11 Have I filled this form in _____ (correct)?

12 I wasn't in a hurry, so I walked _____ (slow) through the park.

13 I closed the door _____ (quiet) when I left.

C Complete the dialogues by putting a suitable adverb into the gaps. Use an adjective from the box to make the adverb.

slow   fast   hard   good (x2)   ~~easy~~   bad

0 A: Were the questions difficult?
   B: No, I answered them __easily__ .

1 A: Does she speak English _____ ?
   B: No, she only knows a few words of English.

2 A: Hurry up! I'm waiting!
   B: Just a minute. I'm coming as _____ as I can.

3 A: Did you lose at tennis again?
   B: Yes, I played _____ and I lost.

4 A: Have you been working _____ today?
   B: No, I've done nothing all day!

5 A: Have you finished that book yet?
   B: No, I always read very _____ . It takes me a long time to finish a book.

6 A: Is he a bad student?
   B: No, he does all his work very _____ .

D Put in the comparative adverb form of the adjective in brackets.

0 You must do your work __more carefully__ (careful) in future.

1 He has run the 100 metres _____ (fast) than any other athlete in the world this year.

2 Everyone else did the test _____ (good) than me.

3 You can travel _____ (cheap) at certain times of the year.

4 He plays _____ (confident) than he did in the past.

5 I'm sorry I've made so many mistakes. I'll try _____ (hard) in future.

6 You will be able to sit _____ (comfortable) in this chair.

41 Adverb + adjective (**very hot**); adjective + adjective; noun + noun (**a cardboard box**)

1

It was cold.　　*It was **very** cold.*

We can use an adverb (e.g. **very**) before an adjective (e.g. **cold**) to make the adjective stronger. Some common adverbs we use in this way are:

very	extremely	really

*We were **very tired** after the trip.*
*I felt **extremely nervous** before the exam.*
*I'm **really angry** with you.* (= very angry)

We can also make an adjective weaker with these adverbs:

fairly	quite

*Our car is **fairly old**.*
　(= It's old, but it isn't very old.)
*The meal was **quite nice**.*
　(= It was nice but not wonderful.)

2 When we use two adjectives together, we order them like this:

▶ We use 'opinion' adjectives (e.g. **wonderful, nice, pleasant, strange**) before any other adjective (e.g. **new**):

OPINION	
a **wonderful,**	new product
a **lovely,**	warm day
a **beautiful,**	little cottage
a **horrible,**	green shirt

▶ We use 'size' adjectives (e.g. **big, tall**) before an adjective that gives other information, for example its age (**new, old**), its colour, its shape (**thin, round**):

SIZE	
a **big,**	new building
a **small,**	red mark
a **huge,**	black cloud
a **large,**	round stone

3 We can use two nouns together. The first noun is like an adjective and gives information about the second noun:

NOUN	+ NOUN
a cardboard	box
a cassette	recorder
a cheque	book
an alarm	clock

Practice

A Complete these sentences using *really* or *quite*.

0 The film was <u>really</u> good. I enjoyed it a lot.

1 It's _____ cold outside, but not very cold.

2 It isn't a wonderful book, but it's _____ good.

3 The tickets were _____ expensive – they cost much more than I expected.

4 This programme is _____ popular in my country; millions of people watch it.

5 He's _____ good at his job, but he sometimes makes bad mistakes.

6 The meal was _____ nice, but it wasn't very good.

7 It's _____ dangerous to drive so fast in such terrible weather conditions.

8 I'm not a very good tennis player, but I am _____ good.

9 They're all _____ intelligent students, and they will all pass their exams easily.

10 The company that I work for is _____ big, but it's not enormous.

B **Put these words into the correct order.**

0 (a – town – beautiful – little)
   <u>a beautiful, little town</u>

1 (a – day – pleasant – sunny)
   _____

2 (a – smile – big – nice)
   _____

3 (a – large – coffee – black)
   _____

4 (a – old – coat – horrible)
   _____

5 (a – large – building – white)
   _____

6 (a – bird – big – grey)
   _____

7 (a – woman – thin – tall)
   _____

8 (a – small – car – blue)
   _____

9 (a – story – little – strange)
   _____

C **Match the words in box A and box B to describe what you can see in each picture.**

A ~~table~~	tennis	paper	B cup	court	pot
photograph	door	soup	handle	sign	hanger
road	air	music	system	bowl	~~lamp~~
coat	coffee	telephone	book	hostess	album

0 <u>a table lamp</u>

1 _____

2 _____

3 _____

4 _____

5 _____

6 _____

7 _____

8 _____

9 _____

10 _____

11 _____

42 Prepositions of place and movement (**in, to** etc.)

1 We can use prepositions to talk about where things or people are. Look at the picture and the examples:

There is somebody **in** the telephone box.
There is a queue of people **outside** the cinema.
The people are standing **on** the pavement.
There is a clock **above** the cinema entrance.
The cinema entrance is **under** the clock.
The bank is **next to** the cinema.
The phone box is **opposite** the cinema.
The bank is **between** the cinema and the café.
There is a hill **behind** the town.
The car is **in front of** the bank.

2 We can also use prepositions to describe movement:

She walked **out of** the house.

I'm flying **to** Italy tomorrow.
I ran **into** the station to catch the train.

He jumped **over** the wall.

She walked **under** the bridge.

We walked **through** the gate.

The cat ran **across** the road. (= from one side to the other side)

We walked **along** the path.

He ran **up** the steps and knocked on the door.
We cycled **down** the hill.

He ran **between** two players and scored a goal.

Practice

A Look at the pictures and put in the correct prepositions in the sentences.

0   1   2   3    4

5   6   7   8    9

0   The file is __on_____ the desk.

1   She's sitting _____ her parents.

2   Do you like the picture _____ the door?

3   He was working _____ his office.

4   The car was parked _____ my house.

5   Where's the waste-paper basket? ~ It's _____ the desk.

6   The woman sitting _____ John on the plane was wearing a big hat.

7   The safe is _____ the picture.

8   They live _____ a caravan.

9   A young man with long hair was sitting _____ him.

B   **Put in the correct prepositions from the box. Use each preposition once.**

under	to	through	down
between	~~along~~	out of	into
across	over	up	

0   She was walking _along_____ the road that goes to the farm.

1   She swam _____ the pool from one side to the other.

2   We ran _____ the hill until we reached the bottom.

3   I climbed _____ the stairs to the top of the building.

4   The dog hid _____ the table, so that we couldn't see it.

5   I jumped _____ the sea and swam to the boat.

6   The horse jumped _____ the last fence and won the race.

7   The vase is _____ the photograph and the clock.

8   The rain came _____ the roof and into the house.

9   I walked _____ the house and went to my car.

10 I went _____ the shops and bought some food.

C   **Put in the correct words from the box. Use each word once.**

behind	outside	in front of	out of	under
over	next to	on	~~into~~	through

0   He picked up the money and put it _into_____ his pocket.

1   The man sitting _____ me was very tall and I couldn't see the game.

2   I keep a lot of useless things on the floor _____ the bed.

3   A fish jumped _____ the water and landed on the shore.

4   I always like to sit _____ the window on aeroplanes, so that I can look at the view.

5   Henry kicked the ball and it went _____ the window and into the kitchen.

6   He was standing _____ me, so I didn't see him.

7   The book that you're looking for is _____ the bottom shelf.

8   The ball went _____ my head, and I couldn't catch it.

9   The manager told me to wait _____ her office because she was talking to someone.

43 Prepositions: **in, with, by, without (by doing)**

1 We can use **in** to describe what somebody is wearing:

*Jane is the woman **in the red dress**.*
*I went to the interview **in my new suit**.*
It was a sunny day, and everyone was in summer clothes.
*Are you allowed to go to work **in jeans**?*
*We saw some soldiers **in uniform**.*

2 We can use **with** to describe a part of somebody's body:

*A small boy **with red hair** came into the shop.*
*Our teacher is a tall man **with a beard**.*
*Lisa is a pretty girl **with blue eyes**.*
*Jack was talking to a man **with a big nose**.*

We can also use **with** to describe animals:

*A rabbit is an animal **with big ears** and a small tail.*

3 We can use **with** to talk about a part of something:

*They live in a white house **with a flat roof**.*
*I bought a shirt **with red stripes**.*
*I used the pot **with the wooden handle**.*
*He has a hi-fi **with very big speakers**.*

4 We can use **with** before something, for example a tool, that we use in order to do something:

*You clean your teeth **with a toothbrush**.*
*You open a tin **with a tin opener**.*
*I cleaned the table **with a cloth**.*
*Please eat **with your knife** and **fork**.*

5 We use **by** + -ing (e.g. **by doing**) to describe how we do or did something:

*She learnt French **by listening** to tapes.*
*You start a car **by turning** the key.*
She became successful in business by working very hard.
*The prisoners escaped **by climbing** over a wall.*

We use **without** + -ing (e.g. **without doing**) to say that a particular action is not done or was not done:

*She passed the exam **without doing** a lot of work.*
*They left **without waiting** for me.*
*He did the work **without making** any mistakes.*

....

Practice

A **Put in the correct prepositions. Use *in* or *with*.**

0   A young man __with__ a moustache was driving the car.

1   He showed me a photograph of a woman _____ blue eyes.

2   We live in a house _____ a green door.

3   A lot of businessmen _____ suits were on the train.

4   There was a plant _____ big, green leaves in the corner of the room.

5   John was walking down the street with a woman _____ a black coat.

6   Look at that bull _____ those enormous horns!

7   One of the children was a girl _____ long, dark hair.

8   A man _____ a hat came into the café.

9   Soldiers _____ uniform were standing at the entrance to the building.

10 She wanted to buy a computer _____ a screen, a keyboard and a mouse.

11 We booked a hotel room _____ a bathroom.

12 It was cold, so I went out _____ a coat and scarf.

13 We've bought a television _____ a big screen.

14 He arrived for the meeting _____ a grey jacket.

B Complete the sentences to describe which of the things in the box the
   people in the pictures are using.

| a spoon | a cloth | ~~a brush~~ |
| a broom | a racquet | a spade |

0 She's painting _with a brush._
1 He's digging _____
2 She's eating _____
3 You play tennis _____ and a ball.
4 He's sweeping the floor _____
5 She's cleaning the cooker _____

C Rewrite each of the following using *by* or *without*.

0 She sat in the corner. She didn't say anything.
   She sat in the corner without saying anything.

0 He opened the door. He turned the key.
   He opened the door by turning the key.

1 He repaired the car. He changed some of the parts.
   _____

2 She answered the question but she didn't read it carefully.
   _____

3 He left. He didn't say thank you.
   _____

4 She got the money because she sold her car.
   _____

5 I threw the letter away. I didn't open it.
   _____

6 We worked all day and we didn't eat anything.
   _____

7 He lost weight. He went on a strict diet.
   _____

8 I went out, but I didn't lock the door.
   _____

44 Relative clauses with **who, which** or **that**

1 Look at this example:
John married a woman.
*John married a woman **who works in his office**.*
We can use **who** or **that** after a person (e.g. **woman**) to say who we are talking about. We call **who works in his office** a relative clause.

Here are some more examples:
*Have you met Jackie? She's the girl **that sits next to Mike in class**.* (Which girl? – The girl that sits next to Mike.)
*I'm very friendly with the people **who live downstairs**.* (Which people? – The people who live downstairs.)

2 If we are talking about a thing or an animal, we use **which** or **that**:
*He took the job **which paid the highest salary**.* (Which job? – The job which paid the highest salary.)
*A kangaroo is an animal **that lives in Australia**.*

3 Notice that we do not say:
*… the people who **they** live downstairs* .
*… an animal that **it** lives in Australia* .

4 Look at this:

Jane is the woman	SUBJECT	
	who	*came for dinner.*
	She	*came for dinner.*

Here, **who** is the subject of the verb (**came**).

Now look at this:

Jackie is the girl	OBJECT	
	who	*you met last week.*
You met	her.	

Here, **who** is the object of the verb (**met**). We can also use **whom** instead of **who** as the object, but this is very unusual now in English:
*She is the girl **whom** you met.*

When **who, which** or **that** are the object, we can leave them out:
Jackie is the girl you met last week.

We do not use a pronoun (e.g. **her, them**) in addition to **who, which** or **that**:
*She is the girl **who** you met **her** last week.*

....

Practice

A Join these sentences using *who* or *which.*

0 We chose the hotel. It seemed to be the nicest.
   We chose the hotel which seemed to be the nicest.

1 She spoke to the man. He was standing next to her.
_____

2 I read the letters. They came in the morning post.
_____

3 He likes the other people. They work in his office.
_____

4 She's that singer. She was on television last night.
_____

5 Next week there is a festival. It happens in the village every summer.
_____

6 I paid the bills. They came yesterday.
_____

B Complete the conversation by putting *who* or *which* into the gaps.

Carol: Did you watch that programme last night?

David: Which one?

Carol: The programme ⁰ which _____ I mentioned a couple of days ago. It's a new series
        ¹_____ started last night.

David: No, I didn't see it. Was it good?

Carol: Yes. It was about a group of friends ²_____ were at school together. Well,
        Rupert . . .

David: Who was Rupert?

Carol: He was an old student of the school ³_____ had become a doctor. He went
        to a party ⁴_____ his old teachers organized. He met a lot of people
        ⁵_____ had been at school with him many years before. They talked about
        the things ⁶_____ they did when they were at school. Then suddenly,
        Rupert saw an old girl-friend ⁷_____ was dancing with John …

David: Don't tell me any more. It's getting too complicated!

C Join these sentences using *who, which* or *that,* as in the example.

0 She chose the books. She wanted to buy them.

   She chose the books that she wanted to buy.

1 We ate the sandwiches. Jack made them.

   _____

2 I'm doing some work. I have to finish it today.

   _____

3 She's an old woman. I often see her when I go to the shops.

   _____

4 He's an actor. A lot of people like him.

   _____

5 It's a magazine. I read it sometimes.

   _____

6 She was wearing a red dress. She wears for parties.

   _____

D Now join these sentences using *who* or *which*, as in the example.

0 The person phoned. He didn't leave a message.

   The person who phoned didn't leave a message.

1 The bus goes to the airport. It leaves every 20 minutes.

   _____

2 The picture was hanging near the door. It was horrible.

   _____

3 The instructor taught me how to drive. He was very patient.

   _____

4 The girl was sitting next to me. She started talking to me.

   _____

Form tables

Table A   Plural nouns

	SINGULAR	PLURAL
+ -s With most nouns we add **-s** to make them plural:	train suitcase radio	trains suitcases radios
+ -es With nouns that end with **-s, -ss, -sh, -ch, -x,** we add **-es**:	bus match box	buses matches boxes
-f/-fe → -ves We change **-f/-fe** to **-ves** in the plural:	loaf life	loaves lives
y → -ies With nouns that end with a consonant* + **-y,** we change the **-y** to **-ies**:	secretary city country	secretaries cities countries
Irregular nouns	man child foot	men children feet

Table B   Present Simple

	I/you/we/they	He/she/it
+ -s After **he/she/it**, we add **-s** to most Present Simple verbs:	work leave use	works leaves uses
+ -es We add **-es** to verbs that end with **-ss, -sh, -ch, -o** (e.g. *finish*, *go*):	pass wash teach **go** **do**	passes washes teaches goes does
y → -ies We change **-y** to **-ies** with verbs that end with a consonant* + **-y**:	**cry** **try** **fly**	cries tries flies

* Consonants: b c d f g h j k l m n p q r s t v w x y z
 Vowels: a e i o u
 Syllables: |*hit*| = 1 syllable; |*vi*|*sit*| = 2 syllables; |*re*|*mem*|*ber*| = 3 syllables

Table C   -ing forms

	INFINITIVE	-ing FORM
+ -ing With most verbs we add -**ing**:	walk read	walk**ing** read**ing**
-e + -ing With verbs that end with a consonant* + -**e**, we delete the -**e** and add -**ing**:	leave take make write	leav**ing** tak**ing** mak**ing** writ**ing**
ie → -ying With verbs that end with -**ie**, we change -**ie** to -**ying**:	lie die	**lying** **dying**
-t → -tting With verbs that end with one vowel* + one consonant (e.g. *sit*, *hit*, *shop*), we double the consonant:	**get** **run** **shop**	**getting** **running** **shopping**
+ -ing But note that we do not double the consonant, (1) when it is a **y** or **w** (e.g. *play*), (2) when the last syllable* is not stressed (e.g. *reMEMber, VISit*):	play snow remember visit listen	play**ing** snow**ing** remember**ing** visit**ing** listen**ing**

Table D   Regular verbs: Past Simple and past participle

	INFINITIVE	PAST SIMPLE	PAST PARTICIPLE
+ -ed With most verbs we add -**ed**:	enjoy finish	enjoy**ed** finish**ed**	enjoy**ed** finish**ed**
+ -d With verbs ending with -**e**, we add -**d**:	close phone	close**d** phone**d**	close**d** phone**d**
y → -ied With verbs that end with a consonant* + -**y**, we change the **y** to -**ied**:	carry marry	carr**ied** marr**ied**	carr**ied** marr**ied**
p → -pped With verbs that end with one vowel* + one consonant (e.g. *stop*), we double the consonant:	**stop** **plan**	**stopped** **planned**	**stopped** **planned**
+ -ed But note that we do not double the consonant, (1) when it is a **y** or **w** (e.g. *stay*), (2) when the last syllable* is not stressed (e.g. *LISten, HAppen, Open*):	**stay** **listen** **happen** **open** **visit**	stay**ed** listen**ed** happen**ed** open**ed** visit**ed**	stay**ed** listen**ed** happen**ed** open**ed** visit**ed**

* Consonants: b c d f g h j k l m n p q r s t v w x y z
Vowels: a e i o u
Syllables: | *hit* | = 1 syllable; | *vi* | *sit* | = 2 syllables; | *re* | *mem* | *ber* | = 3 syllables

Table E   Irregular verbs: Past Simple and past participle

INFINITIVE	PAST SIMPLE	PAST PARTICIPLE	INFINITIVE	PAST SIMPLE	PAST PARTICIPLE
be	was/were	been	lend	lent	lent
become	became	become	let	let	let
begin	began	begun	lose	lost	lost
break	broke	broken	make	made	made
bring	brought	brought	meet	met	met
build	built	built	pay	paid	paid
buy	bought	bought	put	put	put
catch	caught	caught	read	read	read
choose	chose	chosen	ring	rang	rung
come	came	come	run	ran	run
cost	cost	cost	say	said	said
cut	cut	cut	see	saw	seen
do	did	done	sell	sold	sold
drink	drank	drunk	send	sent	sent
drive	drove	driven	show	showed	shown/showed
eat	ate	eaten	shut	shut	shut
fall	fell	fallen	sing	sang	sung
feel	felt	felt	sit	sat	sat
find	found	found	sleep	slept	slept
fly	flew	flown	speak	spoke	spoken
forget	forgot	forgotten	spell	spelt/spelled	spelt/spelled
get	got	got	spend	spent	spent
give	gave	given	stand	stood	stood
go	went	gone	steal	stole	stolen
grow	grew	grown	swim	swam	swum
have	had	had	take	took	taken
hear	heard	heard	teach	taught	taught
hide	hid	hidden	tell	told	told
hit	hit	hit	think	thought	thought
hold	held	held	throw	threw	thrown
hurt	hurt	hurt	understand	understood	understood
keep	kept	kept	wake	woke	woken
know	knew	known	wear	wore	worn
learn	learnt/learned	learnt/learned	win	won	won
leave	left	left	write	wrote	written

Table F Comparative and superlative adjectives

	ADJECTIVE	COMPARATIVE	SUPERLATIVE
+ -er/-est We add -er /-est to short adjectives (one-syllable* adjectives):	warm tall young	warm**er** tall**er** young**er**	the warm**est** the tall**est** the young**est**
+ -r/-st **We** add -r/-st to adjectives that end with -**e**:	late	late**r**	the late**st**
-g → -gger With short adjectives that end with one vowel* and one consonant* (e.g. *big*), we double the consonant:	big hot wet	bi**gg**er ho**tt**er we**tt**er	the bi**gg**est the ho**tt**est the we**tt**est
-w + -er /-est We don't double **w**:	low	low**er**	the low**est**
more/most We use **more / the most** before adjectives of two or more syllables*:	expensive famous beautiful	**more** expensive **more** famous **more** beautiful	the **most** expensive the **most** famous the **most** beautiful
y → -ier/-iest But note that with adjectives ending with -**y** (e.g. *happy*), we change -**y** to -**ier** /-**iest**:	happy lucky easy	happ**ier** luck**ier** eas**ier**	the happ**iest** the luck**iest** the eas**iest**
Irregular adjectives:	good bad far	better worse farther	the best the worst the farthest

Table G Adverbs

	ADJECTIVE	ADVERB
+ -ly With most adverbs, we add -**ly** to the adjective:	quick correct slow	quick**ly** correct**ly** slow**ly**
Exceptions: Adjectives that end with -**y** (**y → -ily**):	happy lucky	happ**ily** luck**ily**
Adjectives that end with -**ble** (-e- + **y**):	remarka**ble**	remarka**bly**
Irregular adverbs	good fast hard late	well fast hard late

* Consonants: b c d f g h j k l m n p q r s t v w x y z
Vowels: a e i o u
Syllables: | *hit* | = 1 syllable; | *vi* | *sit* | = 2 syllables; | *re* | *mem* | *ber* | = 3 syllables

Exit tests

You can do these tests when you have finished studying the units in this book, to see if there are units that you should look at again. In the tests, each question relates to the unit with the same number, e.g. question 1 tests something from unit 1, question 2 tests something from unit 2, etc.

Exit test 1

Choose the right answer (**a**, **b**, or **c**) and write **a**, **b**, or **c** in the box, as in the example. The correct answers are on page 117.

0   Where **a** do   **b** does   **c** is John live?   `b`

1   Ann **a** finishs   **b** finish   **c** finishes work at 6 o'clock.

2   I **a** am makeing   **b** making   **c** 'm making an omelette.

3   Diana **a** is doing   **b** does   **c** do a French course at the moment.

4   We **a** staied   **b** stayyed   **c** stayed in a nice hotel last weekend.

5   He **a** was cook   **b** did cooking   **c** was cooking a meal when I arrived.

6   I **a** know   **b** 've known   **c** am knowing Julia for many years.

7   A parcel **a** just has arrived   **b** has arrived yet   **c** has just arrived for you.

8   We **a** 've arrived   **b** arrived   **c** have arrive at the hotel late last night.

9   I **a** live   **b** 've been living   **c** 'm living here for ten years.

10   I knew her name because I **a** had meet   **b** was met   **c** had met her before.

11   I **a** 'll take   **b** going to take   **c** 'll to take you to the airport.

12   Joan **a** is starting   **b** start   **c** is start her new job next week.

13   If you **a** 'll leave   **b** leave   **c** are leaving soon, you'll catch the 11 o'clock bus.

14   I **a** ask   **b** 'll ask   **c** am asking him to phone you, when he gets home.

15   I like this kind of music. ~ **a** So do I.   **b** I like, too.   **c** So am I.

16   Alison never **a** listens   **b** listens to   **c** listens at the radio.

17   I often **a** do   **b** get   **c** make mistakes when I'm typing.

18   We **a** arrived here yesterday.   **b** here arrived yesterday.   **c** yesterday arrived here.

19   Who **a** went   **b** did go   **c** did they go to the party last night?

20   How **a** far   **b** long   **c** much is it from here to your office? ~ About 2 kilometres.

21   You come from Scotland, **a** don't you?   **b** isn't it?   **c** are you?

22   Excuse me. I **a** must make   **b** must I make   **c** must to make a phone call.

23   She **a** has work   **b** have to work   **c** has to work very hard in her job.

24 You **a** shouldn't eat **b** shouldn't to eat **c** don't should eat so quickly.

25 I **a** couldn't to hear **b** didn't could hear **c** couldn't hear what the man said.

26 This article **a** wrote **b** was written **c** written by a famous journalist.

27 Margaret enjoys **a** learning **b** to learn **c** learn languages.

28 Alan wants **a** work **b** working **c** to work abroad in the future.

29 He said that he **a** post **b** would post **c** will post the letter yesterday.

30 Louise works in **a** the **b** — **c** a shop in New York, but I don't know its name.

31 Mary put a bandage on Tom's finger, because he cut **a** herself **b** him **c** himself when he was preparing the meal.

32 The man **a** offered me **b** to me offered **c** me offered a cigarette.

33 I don't know **a** nothing **b** something **c** anything about the history of Britain.

34 I was at home **a** all day **b** all the day **c** all of day yesterday.

35 I've met **a** both of **b** both the **c** either of her parents and I like them.

36 Frank is **a** taller as **b** taller than **c** more tall than me.

37 My job is **a** as difficult as **b** difficult as **c** as difficult that your job.

38 I didn't go into the museum because it was **a** too expensive. **b** too much expensive. **c** expensive enough.

39 John **a** doesn't interest **b** isn't interested **c** isn't interesting in art.

40 She read the letter **a** careful. **b** carefuly. **c** carefully.

41 I asked for a **a** small, white coffee. **b** coffee small, white. **c** white, small coffee.

42 He walked **a** across **b** through **c** along the road to the other side of the street.

43 She was wearing a T-shirt **a** in **b** by **c** with a red and blue pattern.

44 I stayed with a friend **a** who she lives **b** who lives **c** which lives in the city.

Total:

44

Exit test 2

Choose the right answer (**a**, **b**, **c**) and write **a**, **b**, or **c** in the box, as in the example. The correct answers are on page 117.

0   Who **a** is   **b** do   **c** did   Jane meet?   `c`

1   Jane **a** don't like   **b** doesn't likes   **c** doesn't like   burgers.

2   Carol **a** is writeing   **b** is writting   **c** is writing   a postcard.

3   Lessons **a** are starting   **b** start   **c** are start   at 9 o'clock every morning.

4   The letter **a** came not   **b** didn't came   **c** didn't come   yesterday.

5   Her parents **a** weren't waiting   **b** didn't wait   **c** wasn't waiting   for her when she arrived at the airport.

6   I **a** have visitted   **b** 've visit   **c** 've visited   Africa several times.

7   The post **a** hasn't arrived yet.   **b** already hasn't arrived.   **c** yet hasn't arrived.

8   He's a good friend of mine. I **a** have known   **b** knew   **c** know   him for ten years.

9   Lisa has been learning English **a** for   **b** since   **c** from   two years.

10   When I arrived at the station, the train **a** had left.   **b** has left.   **c** was left.

11   Which film **a** do you go to see   **b** you will see   **c** are you going to see   tonight?

12   When **a** you moving   **b** are you moving   **c** move you   to your new home?

13   You **a** don't have   **b** aren't having   **c** won't have   any money left if you buy that suit.

14   When Mary **a** will get   **b** gets   **c** is getting   here, we'll go out.

15   Michael doesn't speak French and **a** his brother neither.   **b** neither does his brother.   **c** neither his brother.

16   We **a** reached to   **b** reached at   **c** reached   home at 3 a.m.

17   Tina **a** had   **b** got   **c** made   very angry with me.

18   When **a** did you visit China?   **b** did you China visit?   **c** you did visit China?

19   What **a** you saw   **b** saw you   **c** did you see   in Madrid?

20   Susan **a** has 19 years.   **b** is 19.   **c** has 19.

21   I've met you before, **a** didn't I?   **b** did I?   **c** haven't I?

22   I **a** mustn't spend   **b** don't must spend   **c** must not to spend   any more money today.

23   I **a** haven't to get up   **b** don't have to get up   **c** have not get up   early tomorrow, because I'm on holiday.

24 Which bus **a** I should catch? **b** should I to catch? **c** should I catch?

25 I **a** might not go **b** don't might go **c** mightn't to go to the meeting tomorrow.

26 The robber **a** was seen **b** had seen **c** saw by a policeman.

27 I **a** like to go **b** would like to go **c** like going to the cinema tonight.

28 John didn't have a pen, so I let **a** him to borrow **b** him borrow
c that he borrowed mine.

29 Susan **a** told **b** said me **c** told me that she had enjoyed her holiday.

30 Stuart is a vegetarian. He doesn't eat **a** — **b** the **c** a meat.

31 We enjoyed **a** ourselves **b** us **c** ourself a lot on our holiday.

32 A friend **a** to me lent **b** me lent **c** lent me some money.

33 I'm hungry because I haven't eaten **a** anything **b** nothing **c** something all day.

34 **a** None of **b** None of the **c** None shops were open, so we couldn't buy any food.

35 She asked Mark and Trudy, but they couldn't help her because **a** either of **b** neither of
c both them knew the answer.

36 He is **a** best **b** the best **c** the better player in the team.

37 I haven't visited **a** as many countries than **b** as much countries as
c as many countries as you have.

38 We couldn't go into the museum because we didn't have **a** money enough.
b too many money. **c** enough money.

39 There is nothing to do in this town. I'm **a** bored. **b** bore. **c** boring.

40 Linda speaks Spanish **a** better as **b** better than **c** best than I do.

41 I work in a **a** modern, tall building. **b** tall, modern building.
c building tall modern.

42 They climbed **a** over **b** in **c** between the wall and landed on the other side.

43 We drove 300 kilometres without **a** stop. **b** stopping. **c** to stop.

44 This is the book **a** that we used **b** which did we use **c** which we used it on the
course.

Total:

44

Answer key to practice exercises

Unit 1

A
1 rains
2 don't drive
3 has
4 doesn't earn
5 doesn't happen
6 flies
7 leave
8 don't do
9 reads
10 don't listen
11 arrives
12 go

B
1 Does Carol work
2 do you play
3 Do you take
4 do the shops close?
5 Do you go
6 Do you drink
7 does he drive?
8 do the lessons finish?

C
1 takes
2 have
3 eat
4 teaches
5 Do you come
6 does the post arrive
7 don't play
8 Does she go
9 do you park

Unit 2

A
1 They're carrying
2 She's taking
3 They're sitting
4 They're running
5 He's writing

B
1 is/'s he doing
2 Are you listening
3 are you going
4 is/'s he cooking
5 is/'s she staying
6 Are you waiting
7 Is it raining
8 are you reading

C
1 They're playing
2 Is the weather getting
3 Are you leaving
4 He's/He is making
5 It isn't/It's not/It is not working
6 Are you watching
7 He's/He is posting
8 Is Paul doing

Unit 3

A
1 works …'s/is doing
2 washes
3 tries … plays
4 're/are sitting
5 Do you listen
6 'm/am writing
7 do they drive
8 doesn't get
9 rains … isn't/'s not raining
10 'm/am baking … are you smiling … Am I doing?

B
1 I don't know. I'm waiting for the 6.15 to Brussels. And you?
2 Yes, me too. Do you live in Brussels?
3 No. I come from Brussels, but I'm studying at university in Paris at the moment.
4 Oh yes? What course are you taking?
5 I'm doing a two-year course in Business Management.
6 So why are you going to Brussels?
7 All my friends live there and I often go there at weekends.
8 I don't know many people in Paris. What about you? Do you often go to Brussels?
9 Yes, on business. I'm going to a meeting there today.
10 Oh yes. What kind of job do you do?
11 I work in the Marketing Department of a small company, and I often travel to different towns and cities for meetings.
12 What does your company sell?
13 It makes clocks.
14 Oh look! The train is coming.

Unit 4

A
1. took
2. walked ... played
3. Was your meal ... wasn't ... didn't like
4. said ... didn't hear
5. rang ... opened
6. wrote ... posted
7. Did you understand ... tried ... spoke
8. didn't go ... was
9. Did you buy ... bought
10. Did you enjoy ... didn't rain ... was

B
1. When did you finish your exams?
2. I waited for an hour, but he didn't phone.
3. Did you watch the news on TV last night?
4. Mark stopped smoking last month, and he started playing tennis again last week.
5. He asked me a question, but I didn't know the answer.
6. I lived there for a few years, but I didn't like the place.
7. She came to my house yesterday, but she didn't stay.
8. What did you say? I didn't hear you.
9. What did you do yesterday? Did you go to school?

C
1. took
2. Was it
3. bought
4. was
5. Did you go
6. came
7. did you visit
8. went
9. had
10. loved
11. did you like
12. was
13. took
14. did you arrive

Unit 5

A
1. wasn't listening
2. was talking
3. were waiting
4. was living
5. was coming
6. were winning
7. were sitting
8. were you staying
9. wasn't driving
10. wasn't raining
11. were you doing

B
1. was eating
2. were playing
3. was watching
4. was sitting
5. was writing
6. was brushing
7. was listening
8. was painting

C
1. was living
2. was studying
3. was doing
4. left ... was working
5. met ... was working
6. was working ... met
7. was running
8. was running ... married

Unit 6

A
1. has/'s lived.
2. has/'s visited
3. has/'s been
4. has/'s written
5. has/'s climbed

B
1. haven't/have not read
2. 've/have lost
3. 's/has bought
4. 've/have booked
5. 've/have made
6. hasn't/has not happened
7. Have you replied

C
1. Yes, in fact I have worked abroad.
2. I've worked in Ireland and Brazil.
3. What about you? Have you ever had a job abroad?
4. No, I've never wanted to leave my home town.
5. I've lived here for twenty years, and I've never thought of working abroad.
6. Really? Well, I've applied for another job abroad.

D
1. I've/I have known her for more than ten years .
2. I haven't eaten anything since lunchtime.
3. Have you lived in this town for a long time?
4. Jill has been a good friend since we were at school together.
5. Have you seen Jack since the party last week?

Unit 7

A 1 I've/I have just come
   2 I've/I have just sold
   3 She's/She has just finished
   4 I've/I have just had
   5 they've/they have just moved
   6 I've/I have just bought
   7 I've/I have just had

B 1 Have you decided which one to buy yet?
   2 I've/I have already explained this to you three times.
   3 Their baby son has already started talking.
   4 Have you phoned Jane yet?
   5 The game hasn't finished yet.
   6 I've/I have already had lunch.
   7 He's/He has already spent all his money.

C 1 Have you visited the Art Gallery yet?
   2 I haven't done that yet
   3 Have you seen a play yet?
   4 I've just booked a ticket
   5 I've already seen that play.
   6 I've just read
   7 They've just made
   8 they haven't sold all the tickets yet.

Unit 8

A 1 I went
   2 Did you like
   3 I enjoyed
   4 did you do
   5 I visited
   6 Have you been
   7 I've booked

B 1 haven't seen
   2 went
   3 Did you enjoy
   4 was
   5 have never heard
   6 have been
   7 did you do
   8 stayed
   9 needed
   10 Have you ever won
   11 won
   12 Did you meet
   13 have been

C 1 started
   2 built
   3 went
   4 pulled
   5 have opened
   6 opened
   7 went
   8 opened
   9 began
   10 have built

Unit 9

A 1 It's/It has been raining since 3 o'clock.
   2 He's/He has been playing chess since he was 10.
   3 I've/I have been working since 8 o'clock.
   4 Helen's/Helen has been looking for another job for two months.
   5 We've/We have been waiting (here) for two hours.

B 1 for   5 since
   2 for   6 since
   3 since   7 for
   4 for   8 for

C 1 've/have been staying
   2 've/have been waiting
   3 's/has been talking
   4 've/have been having
   5 have you been looking
   6 've/have been applying

D 1 's/has been raining
   2 've/have been playing
   3 's/has been studying
   4 've/have been reading
   5 've/have been watching
   6 have been making
   7 've/have been saving

Unit 10

A 1 hadn't/had not booked
   2 had spent
   3 had got up
   4 hadn't/had not done
   5 had won
   6 had forgotten
   7 had left
   8 hadn't/had not heard
   9 had disappeared
   10 hadn't/had not brought
   11 hadn't/had not rained

B 1 he had cleaned the flat.
2 he hadn't/he had not bought anything to drink.
3 he had had a shower.
4 he had changed his clothes.
5 he had started preparing the meal.
6 he hadn't/he had not finished preparing the meal.

C 1 When I had done the course, I was able to speak the language well.
2 When he had done all his work, he went home.
3 When everyone had left, I went to bed.
4 When she had had a glass of water, she felt better.
5 When he had done the washi~
 listened to some mu~
6 When Steve ~
 bou~
7 ... I~
 frie~
8 ... ~
 spea~
9 ... tic~

Unit 11

A 1 's/is going~
2 's/is going ~
3 's/is going t~
4 's/is going to~
5 's/is going to ~

B 1 I'll give you a l~
2 I'll phone you t~
3 I'll buy the ticket~
 meet you at the c~
4 I'll lend you my un~

C 1 are going to have
2 'm/am going to play
3 're/are going to move
4 's/is going to look
5 's/is going to rain

D 1 I'm/I am going to watch
2 are you going to eat ... I'll ~
3 I'm/I am going to buy ... are you going to get ... I'm/I am going to look ... I'll come
4 I'm/I am going to leave ... I'll see
5 I'm/I am going to phone
6 I'm/I am going to travel

Unit 12

A 1 We're flying
2 We're staying
3 We're visiting
4 We're taking
5 We're having
6 We're seeing
7 We're leaving

B 1 She's going
2 She's playing
3 She's going
4 She's having
5 She's meeting
6 She's seeing
7 are going/coming
8 She isn't/'s not/is not doing

1 I'm going
 are you catching
 I'm meeting
 are you meeting
 ~e're meeting
 ~'re going
 ~ having
 ~ou doing
 ~elping
 ~u coming
 ~ching

~egetarian, you don't eat meat.
~ a hot country, you don't like

~her, you have to work very

~ exercise, you stay fit and

~ic, you understand

~spapers, you know what's
~ing in the world.

1 the weather is ... we'll drive
2 she posts ... they'll receive
3 The boss will be ... John arrives
4 I'll go ... I have
5 she doesn't pass ... she won't get
6 You'll learn ... you take
7 I get ... I'll go
8 I'll buy ... it doesn't cost
9 you run ... you'll catch
10 I'll go ... I don't feel
11 they win ... they'll be

C 1 I'll buy … I go
   2 doesn't phone … I'll phone
   3 you want … I'll give
   4 he'll fail … he doesn't work
   5 you fill in … I'll send

Unit 14

A 1 until
   2 when
   3 When
   4 after/when
   5 until
   6 until
   7 when
   8 As soon as/When
   9 until
  10 When
  11 before
  12 as soon as
  13 before

B 1 'll wait … arrive
   2 'll see … go
   3 'll phone … know
   4 'll do … have
   5 'll enjoy … get
   6 'll tell … see
   7 'll wait … comes
   8 'll book … go
   9 'll do … get
  10 Will you see … 're/are … 'll phone … arrive

C 1 'll pay
   2 'll ask
   3 has landed/lands
   4 've/have checked
   5 'll read
   6 've/have read
   7 'll feel
   8 've/have finished
   9 'll be
  10 've/have had

Unit 15

A 1 Neither
   2 Neither
   3 So
   4 Neither
   5 too
   6 So
   7 so
   8 neither
   9 too
  10 either
  11 so
  12 neither

B 1 So are we.
   2 Neither does mine.
   3 Neither have I.
   4 So was mine.
   5 So has Frank.
   6 Neither did George.
   7 Neither can I.
   8 Neither am I.
   9 So did John.
  10 So have I.
  11 So are we.
  12 So is mine.

C 1 neither does
   2 doesn't either
   3 so does
   4 does too
   5 neither can
   6 can't either
   7 can too
   8 neither can
   9 so has
  10 so does
  11 does too
  12 so does
  13 neither does

Unit 16

A
1 for
2 to
3 for
4 —
5 —
6 —
7 —
8 on
9 —
10 with
11 for
12 to

B
1 for
2 —
3 about
4 —
5 for
6 with
7 on

C
1 to
2 talking about
3 applied for
4 are you waiting for
5 are you looking for
6 did she ask for

D
1 at
2 —
3 for
4 to
5 for
6 at
7 —
8 —

Unit 17

A
1 gets
2 get
3 do
4 made
5 did
6 got
7 gets
8 make
9 make
10 made
11 getting
12 got

B
1 had/made
2 had
3 got
4 got
5 did
6 had
7 had
8 done
9 did
10 had
11 did

C
1 do
2 made
3 got
4 had
5 made
6 have
7 do

Unit 18

A
1 Where did you put my coat?
2 We took a taxi from the airport.
3 She started the job three weeks ago.
4 Two friends and I travelled around Europe last summer.
5 Are you going to Italy tomorrow?
6 When did you visit Egypt?

B
1 He brought a letter.
2 It was a letter from Maria and her son Matthew.
3 I read it before I went to work.
4 They are coming here next week.
5 I am going to meet them at the airport on Tuesday.
6 They are going to stay at my house.
7 She takes her son abroad every year.
8 She took him to France last year.
9 I'm going to visit her next year.

C
1 did you see
2 you speak any foreign languages?
3 are you working
4 did you start there?
5 you use a computer?
6 Do you like the job?
7 are you leaving (it)?
8 When can you start?

Unit 19

A 1 Who wants some more coffee?
  2 What happened at the end of the story?
  3 Who is going to pay the bill?
  4 What did he have for breakfast?
  5 What did their letter say?
  6 Who knows the answer to my question?
  7 What did they see?
  8 Who is she phoning?

B 1 Who went on the trip?
  2 What's happening in this film?
  3 Who are you going to phone?
  4 What did you watch on TV last night?
  5 Who sent these flowers?
  6 What did you buy in that shop?
  7 What has made Tom so happy?

C 1 What happened?
  2 Who took his driving test?
  3 What did Robert fail?
  4 Who did Robert meet afterwards?
  5 What did Robert say to Philip?
  6 What did Philip say to Robert?
  7 Who did Philip meet for coffee?
  8 What did Philip say to Linda?
  9 What did Linda do?

Unit 20

A 1 How often does he read a newspaper?
  2 How much does a single room cost?
  3 How old were you when you went to live in Australia?
  4 How many exams are you going to take?
  5 How long will the course last?
  6 How far is it from here to the nearest bus stop?

B 1 How many languages do/can you speak?
  2 How far is it …?
  3 How much did the meal cost?
  4 How long did you stay …?
  5 How often does the postman come?
  6 How much cheese did you buy?

C 1 from … to/until
  2 every
  3 much
  4 from … to
  5 years old
  6 many

D 1 How often do you go there?
  2 How long do the lessons last?

  3 How often do you study at home?
  4 How many people are there in your class?
  5 How old are they?
  6 How far is it from your home?
  7 How much does it cost?

Unit 21

A 1 don't you
  2 isn't it
  3 does it
  4 don't they
  5 have you
  6 aren't you

B 1 can't I
  2 will it
  3 was he
  4 did I
  5 will it
  6 wasn't it
  7 can you
  8 didn't they

C 1 isn't it
  2 haven't you
  3 can you
  4 don't they
  5 won't I

D 1 You can speak French (very well), can't you?
  2 You haven't heard this story, have you?
  3 You went to Frank's party, didn't you?
  4 It isn't very far from here, is it?
  5 She won't be angry, will she?
  6 You're not going to leave now, are you?
  7 You'll be at home tonight, won't you?

Unit 22

A 1 mustn't/must not take
  2 You must pay
  3 You must vacate
  4 You mustn't/must not smoke
  5 You must return

B 1 mustn't forget
  2 must go
  3 mustn't worry
  4 must book
  5 must lock
  6 must see
  7 must phone

C 1 You mustn't take
    2 You mustn't make
    3 You mustn't write
    4 You must arrive
    5 You must bring

D 1 mustn't/must not tell lies
    2 must not/mustn't open the door
    3 must come for dinner with us
    4 must show identity cards
    5 mustn't/must not eat
    6 must follow the instructions
    7 must write

Unit 23

A 1 don't have to deal with
    2 don't have to be polite
    3 have to be polite
    4 have to work
    5 have to work
    6 don't have to work
    7 have to wear
    8 don't have to wear

B 1 I didn't have to work
    2 Do I have to do
    3 I had to run
    4 I had to go
    5 Did you have to show
    6 Do/Will I have to pay
    7 do you have to have
    8 You don't/won't have to decide
    9 I had to wait
   10 Do you have to work … I had to work

C 1 You have to fill in an application form.
    2 Do I have to give you a photograph?
    3 No, you don't have to give me anything, except the money for the card!
    4 We had to do some English tests.
    5 How many questions did you have to answer?
    6 We had to answer about 40 grammar questions.
    7 I had to think about them very carefully.
    8 Did you have to write a composition?
    9 No, but we'll have to/we have to do one next week.

Unit 24

A 1 You shouldn't park
    2 should I cook
    3 You should wear
    4 You shouldn't smoke
    5 We should arrive
    6 Should I pay
    7 I should apply
    8 I should write
    9 I shouldn't eat
   10 We should complain
   11 I should buy

B 1 You should cut
    2 You should use
    3 You shouldn't put
    4 You should wait
    5 You should heat
    6 You should cut

C 1 Which papers should I get?
    2 I think you should buy the local newspapers.
    3 What do you think I should do before I buy a bike?
    4 I don't think you should decide too quickly.
    5 You should check the condition of the bike.
    6 You should ask somebody who knows about bikes to look at the bike for you.
    7 You shouldn't buy one simply because it looks nice!
    8 You should be very careful.

Unit 25

A 1 couldn't play
    2 can't cook
    3 can't give
    4 couldn't see
    5 can do
    6 can play
    7 can't find
    8 couldn't understand
    9 couldn't go … couldn't afford
   10 couldn't do
   11 can't talk

B 1 She can't see anything without her glasses.
    2 She was so tired after the race that she couldn't stand up.
    3 Last year, Robert could beat his younger brother at chess.
    4 They can see the whole of the city.

C
1 might buy
2 might be
3 might go
4 might not go
5 might not come
6 might stay
7 might be ... might be
8 might not be
9 might not be
10 might find

D
1 may not be
2 may not go
3 may stay
4 may watch
5 may get

Unit 26

A
1 is delivered
2 is served
3 isn't/is not used
4 are held
5 is your name spelt
6 are sold
7 is paid
8 are made
9 is taken
10 is not known
11 is shown
12 are paid

B
1 was written
2 was answered
3 was made
4 was tennis invented
5 wasn't/was not injured
6 was born
7 was this pot made
8 was this city built
9 was painted
10 was this book published
11 was given

C
1 The electric light bulb was invented by Thomas Edison.
2 The office was painted last week.
3 The accident was seen by several people.
4 Where are these video recorders made?
5 The agreement was signed by six countries.
6 I was helped by a stranger.
7 The post isn't/is not delivered on Sundays.

D
1 produced
2 were exported
3 started
4 were tested
5 was called
6 exported
7 are sold

Unit 27

A
1 stop running
2 don't mind listening
3 keeps losing
4 enjoys going ... likes meeting
5 keep making
6 finish eating
7 doesn't enjoy driving ... loves cycling
8 Do you like reading
9 don't mind changing
10 stop making

B
1 like living
2 would like to be
3 don't like getting up
4 'd/would like to go out
5 would like to find
6 don't like watching
7 likes lying
8 would/'d like to discuss
9 Would you like to come
10 'd/would like to do
11 likes going
12 doesn't like cooking
13 Does she like working ... 'd/would like to find
14 would you like to do ... 'd/would like to visit

C 1 he went dancing.
　　2 he went cycling.
　　3 he went swimming.
　　4 he went skiing.
　　5 he went sailing.

Unit 28

A 1 to phone
　　2 be
　　3 work
　　4 enjoy
　　5 to wait
　　6 to eat
　　7 reply
　　8 feel
　　9 leave
　　10 to bring
　　11 receive

B 1 come to the meeting on Friday.
　　2 to meet some friends tonight.
　　3 to listen to what I'm telling you.
　　4 to lock the door when you go out.
　　5 go out for a meal this evening.
　　6 me pay for the meal.
　　7 to do a course in Art History.
　　8 to pay the bill.
　　9 to sit in this chair?
　　10 me laugh (a lot).
　　11 phone you tomorrow.
　　12 be angry with you.
　　13 me drive her new car.

C 1 do
　　2 to go
　　3 to come
　　4 to leave
　　5 to start
　　6 to take
　　7 to reach
　　8 meet
　　9 be

Unit 29

A 1 (that) she was going to a conference.
　　2 (that) he'd/he had lost his passport.
　　3 (that) they'd/they had been on holiday.
　　4 (that) she didn't understand.
　　5 (that) they were staying for three weeks.

B 1 (that) she was enjoying
　　2 (that) she had been
　　3 (that) she was
　　4 (that) she was staying
　　5 (that) they/her friends had
　　6 (that) she was leaving
　　7 (that) she couldn't speak
　　8 (that) she was going to have
　　9 (that) she would teach

C 1 told
　　2 said
　　3 told
　　4 told
　　5 told
　　6 told
　　7 said
　　8 said
　　9 told
　　10 told … told

Unit 30

A 1 a … —
　　2 — … —
　　3 a … the
　　4 — … a
　　5 an … the
　　6 a … a
　　7 — … an … the
　　8 a … —

B 1 — … the
　　2 the
　　3 a … the
　　4 —
　　5 — … —
　　6 a … the
　　7 —
　　8 —
　　9 — … the
　　10 the … the
　　11 the … the … the
　　12 —

C 1 an　　　　7 —
　　2 a　　　　 8 a
　　3 —　　　　9 the
　　4 the　　　10 a
　　5 a　　　　11 the
　　6 a　　　　12 —

D 1 a
2 the
3 a
4 the
5 the
6 a
7 a
8 the
9 the

Unit 31

A 1 himself
2 myself
3 ourselves
4 themselves
5 himself
6 himself

B 1 enjoyed ourselves very much.
2 burnt myself
3 He taught himself.
4 I think I'm going to buy/I'll buy myself a new coat tomorrow.
5 She made herself a sandwich

C 1 myself
2 herself
3 themselves
4 ourselves
5 himself

D 1 You'll have to post it yourself.
2 we carried all our luggage ourselves.
3 Did you take it yourself?
4 she (had) made herself.
5 I chose it myself.
6 I invented the recipe myself.

E 1 each other
2 each other
3 yourselves
4 ourselves
5 each other
6 each other

Unit 32

A 1 She offered Jim a cigarette.
2 He showed Mary his holiday photographs.
3 Have you sent them an invitation?
4 Did you buy her a birthday present?
5 I gave a friend some of my tapes.
6 When you go to the post office, could you get me some stamps?

B 1 She offered a cigarette to Jim.
2 He showed his holiday photographs to Mary.
3 Have you sent an invitation to them?
4 Did you buy a birthday present for her?
5 I gave some of my tapes to a friend.
6 When you go to the post office, could you get some stamps for me?

C 1 I have sent a birthday card to Jane.
2 I don't want to lend Bruce my bike.
3 I gave Joan your message.
4 Could you fetch a knife and fork for me?

D 1 The waiter fetched them some wine. ... The waiter fetched some wine for them.
2 The waiter showed him the bottle. ... The waiter showed the bottle to Tim.
3 The chef cooked them a special meal. ... The chef cooked a special meal for them.
4 The waiter gave Tim the bill. ... The waiter gave the bill to Tim.
5 Lucy lent Tim some money, because he didn't have enough to pay the bill. ... Lucy lent some money to Tim, because he didn't have enough to pay the bill.

Unit 33

A 1 nobody
2 anything
3 somewhere
4 nobody
5 nothing
6 something
7 nothing
8 nothing ... anything
9 anywhere ... somewhere

B 1 knew
2 haven't seen
3 didn't eat
4 has happened
5 is
6 didn't say

C 1 anything interesting
  2 anywhere else
  3 anywhere cheap
  4 somewhere else
  5 something hot

D 1 somebody/someone
  2 somebody/someone
  3 something
  4 anybody/anyone
  5 anywhere
  6 anything
  7 Something

Unit 34

A 1 all of the
  2 none of
  3 some of the
  4 some of
  5 some of
  6 none of
  7 none of the
  8 all of the

B 1 all the
  2 all
  3 Some of the
  4 Some
  5 None of the
  6 all
  7 None of the
  8 all
  9 None of the
  10 All
  11 all
  12 none of the
  13 Some of the

C 1 most of … all of it
  2 most of … all of it
  3 all of … most of them
  4 all of … none of them
  5 None of … all of them
  6 all of … none of it

Unit 35

A 1 either
  2 Neither
  3 Neither … either
  4 either
  5 neither
  6 either … neither
  7 either
  8 neither
  9 either
  10 either
  11 neither
  12 either

B 1 Both of them
  2 Neither of them
  3 Both of them
  4 Neither of them
  5 Both of them
  6 Neither of them

C 1 either of them
  2 both of them
  3 neither of them
  4 both of us
  5 neither of us
  6 neither of us
  7 either of them
  8 Both of us
  9 both of them

Unit 36

A 1 taller than
  2 older than
  3 richer than
  4 lower than
  5 bigger than
  6 smaller than

B 1 easier than
  2 better than
  3 more successful than
  4 luckier than
  5 more powerful than
  6 more useful than

C 1 the worst
  2 the funniest
  3 the tallest
  4 the best
  5 the most expensive
  6 the most beautiful

D 1 the happiest
2 more famous than
3 worse than
4 the best
5 the most expensive
6 more difficult than
7 wetter than
8 more comfortable than
9 the most exciting . . . more exciting than

Unit 37

A 1 as quickly as
2 as angry as
3 as expensive as
4 as big as
5 as good as
6 as hard as

B 1 as fast as
2 as tall as
3 as long as
4 as clean as
5 as fresh as
6 as full as
7 as strong as
8 as wide as
9 as big as

C 1 as much (money) as
2 as many countries as
3 as many jobs as
4 as much luggage as
5 as many questions as
6 as much (money) as

Unit 38

A 1 too dark
2 enough information
3 too late
4 enough food
5 too nervous
6 too fast
7 good enough
8 enough clothes
9 well enough
10 strong enough
11 too cold
12 enough stamps

B 1 enough time
2 too many questions
3 warm enough
4 too much salt
5 enough questions
6 too many people
7 comfortable enough
8 too much noise
9 enough players
10 enough bread
11 too many mistakes

C 1 I'm too tired to do any more work.
2 Judy isn't good enough to pass the exam.
3 Clive is too short to play basketball. / Clive isn't tall enough to play basketball.
4 His girl-friend was too ill to go to the party. / His girl-friend wasn't well enough to go to the party.
5 David didn't have enough money to pay the bill.
6 Is it hot enough to go to the beach?
7 I'm too busy to see you tonight.
8 It's too early to go home.
9 Chris didn't have enough tools to repair the car.
10 I didn't have enough time to visit all the museums.

Unit 39

A 1 excited
2 surprised
3 interesting
4 tiring
5 surprised
6 bored
7 exciting
8 boring

B 1 amusing
2 boring
3 interested
4 confusing
5 bored
6 amused
7 confused
8 surprising
9 surprised

C 1 bored
2 disappointing
3 disappointed
4 boring
5 surprised
6 confused
7 surprising
8 disappointing
9 boring

Unit 40

A 1 slowly
2 quickly
3 immediate
4 bad
5 badly
6 well
7 good
8 polite
9 politely

B 1 carefully
2 angrily
3 easily
4 fast
5 badly
6 hard
7 busily
8 beautifully
9 happily
10 hard
11 correctly
12 slowly
13 quietly

C 1 well
2 fast
3 badly
4 hard
5 slowly
6 well

D 1 faster
2 better
3 more cheaply
4 more confidently
5 harder
6 more comfortably

Unit 41

A 1 quite
2 quite
3 really
4 really
5 quite
6 quite
7 really
8 quite
9 really
10 quite

B 1 a pleasant, sunny day
2 a nice, big smile
3 a large, black coffee
4 a horrible, old coat
5 a large, white building
6 a big, grey bird
7 a tall, thin woman
8 a small, blue car
9 a strange, little story

C 1 a coffee pot
2 a photograph album
3 a tennis court
4 a road sign
5 a door handle
6 an air hostess
7 a music system
8 a telephone book
9 a coat hanger
10 a paper cup
11 a soup bowl

Unit 42

A 1 between
2 above
3 in
4 in front of/outside
5 under
6 next to
7 behind
8 in
9 opposite

B 1 across
   2 down
   3 up
   4 under
   5 into
   6 over
   7 between
   8 through
   9 out of
  10 to

C 1 in front of
   2 under
   3 out of
   4 next to
   5 through
   6 behind
   7 on
   8 over
   9 outside

Unit 43

A 1 with
   2 with
   3 in
   4 with
   5 in
   6 with
   7 with
   8 in
   9 in
  10 with
  11 with
  12 in
  13 with
  14 in

B 1 with a spade.
   2 with a spoon.
   3 with a racquet
   4 with a broom.
   5 with a cloth.

C 1 He repaired the car by changing some of the parts.
   2 She answered the question without reading it carefully.
   3 He left without saying thank you.
   4 She got the money by selling her car.
   5 I threw the letter away without opening it.
   6 We worked all day without eating anything.
   7 He lost weight by going on a strict diet.
   8 I went out without locking the door.

Unit 44

A 1 She spoke to the man who was standing next to her.
   2 I read the letters which came in the morning post.
   3 He likes the other people who work in his office.
   4 She's that singer who was on television last night.
   5 Next week there is a festival which happens in the village every summer.
   6 I paid the bills which came yesterday.

B 1 which
   2 who
   3 who
   4 which
   5 who
   6 which
   7 who

C 1 We ate the sandwiches which/that Jack made.
   2 I'm doing some work which/that I have to finish today.
   3 She's an old woman who/that I often see when I go to the shops.
   4 He's an actor who/that a lot of people like.
   5 It's a magazine which/that I read sometimes.
   6 She was wearing a red dress which/that she wears at parties.

D 1 The bus which goes to the airport leaves every 20 minutes.
   2 The picture which was hanging near the door was horrible.
   3 The instructor who taught me how to drive was very patient.
   4 The girl who was sitting next to me started talking to me.

Answer key to exit test 1

1	c	12	a	23	c	34	a
2	c	13	b	24	a	35	a
3	a	14	b	25	c	36	b
4	c	15	a	26	b	37	a
5	c	16	b	27	a	38	a
6	b	17	c	28	c	39	b
7	c	18	a	29	b	40	c
8	b	19	a	30	a	41	a
9	b	20	a	31	c	42	a
10	c	21	a	32	a	43	c
11	a	22	a	33	c	44	b

Answer key to exit test 2

1	c	12	b	23	b	34	b
2	c	13	c	24	c	35	b
3	b	14	b	25	a	36	b
4	c	15	b	26	a	37	c
5	a	16	c	27	b	38	c
6	c	17	b	28	b	39	a
7	a	18	a	29	c	40	b
8	a	19	c	30	a	41	b
9	a	20	b	31	a	42	a
10	a	21	c	32	c	43	b
11	c	22	a	33	a	44	a

Index

The numbers in the index are unit numbers. They are not page numbers.

A

a 30
above 42
across 42
adjectives 18
   adjective + adjective (*nice, new*) 41
   adverb + adjective (*very new*) 41
   as + adjective + **as** 37
   comparative and superlative 36, Table F
   -ed or **-ing** 39
   order 41
   with **something, anybody, nobody**, etc. 33
   with **too** and **enough** 38
adverbs 40, Table G
   as + adverb + **as** 37
   comparative 40
   irregular 40
   regular 40
age 20
after 14
agree 16, 28
all 34
along 42
already 7
an 30
answer 16
anything / anybody / anyone / anywhere 33
apply for 16
arrange 28
arrive at / in 16
articles 30
ask for 16
as
   as + adjective / adverb + **as** 37
   as much / many as 37
as soon as 14

B

before 6, 10, 14
be going to 11, 12
behind 42
belong to 16
better 36, 40
between 42
both 35
buy 32

by

   + **ing** 43
   with passive 26

C

can 25
comparative adjectives 36, Table F
comparative adverbs 40
conditional 13
conjunctions (time) 14
cook 32
could 25

D

decide 28
depend on 16
direction
   prepositions 42
   word order 18
direct object 32
discuss 16
do 17
down 42

E

each other 31
either 15, 35
else 33
enjoy 27
enough 38
ever 6
extremely 41

F

fairly 41
fast 40
fetch 32
finish 27
first conditional 13
for 4, 6, 9
forget 28
from
   from . . . to (distance) 20
   from . . . to/until (time) 20
future
   be going to 11, 12
   present continuous 12
   present simple 13, 14
   will 11
   with **if** 13
   with **when / until / before / after / as soon as** 14

G

get 17, 32
give 32
go + **-ing** 27
going to 11, 12
good / better / well 36, 40, Tables F & G

H

had 10
hard 40
have 17
have to 23
herself 31
himself 31
hope 28
how
   how far? 20
   how long? 9, 20
   how many? 20
   how much? 20
   how often? 20
   how old? 20

I

if 13
in
   in and **with** 43
   place 42
indirect object 32
infinitive (with / without **to**) 28
in front of 42
-ing
   adjectives ending with **-ing** 39
   go + **-ing** 27
   -ing forms 2, Table C
   preposition + **-ing** 43
   verb + **-ing** 27
into 42
irregular adverbs 40, Table G
irregular verbs 4, Table E
itself 31

J

just 7

K

keep 27

L

lend 32
less 36

let 28
like
   like + -ing 27
   like / would like 27
listen to 16
look at / for 16
love 27

M

make 17, 28
many 20, 37
may 25
might 25
mind (verb) 27
modals 22, 24, 25, 28
more 36
most 34, 36
much 20, 37
must 22
myself 31

N

neither 15, 35
never 6
next to 42
none 34
nor 35
nothing / nobody / no one
   / nowhere 33
nouns
   noun + noun 41
   plural Table A
   uncountable 20, 30, 37, 38
   with as much / as many
     37
   with too and enough 38
   with/without articles 30
   word order 18

O

object
   direct and indirect 32
   questions 19
   word order 18
offer 28, 32
on 42
opposite 42
ourselves 31
out of 42
outside 42
over 42

P

passive 26
past continuous 5, 29
past participle 6, 7, 10,
   Table D, Table E
past perfect 10

past simple 4, 8
   Table D, Table E
past simple passive 26
pay 16
phone 16
place
   prepositions 42
   word order 18
plan 28
plural nouns Table A
prepositions
   at the end of questions 16
   by + -ing 43
   for 4
   for / since 6, 9
   from . . . to (distance) 20
   from . . . to / until (time) 20
   in and with 43
   + -ing 43
   movement 42
   place 42
   with 43
   with verbs 16
   without + -ing 43
present continuous 2, 3, 12
present perfect 6, 7, 8
present perfect continuous 9
present simple 1, 3
   Table B
present simple passive 26
promise 28
pronouns
   omission in relative clauses
     44
   reflexive and emphatic 31

Q

questions 19, 20
question tags 21
quite 41

R

reach 16
really 41
reflexive and emphatic pronouns
   31
regular adverbs 40, Table G
regular verbs 4, 6, Table D
relative clauses 44
reported speech 29
ring 16

S

say 29
seem 18
send 32
sentence structure 18
should 24

show 32
since 6, 9
so . . . I 15
some 34
something / somebody /
   somewhere 33
stop 27
subject 18
superlative adjectives 36, Table F

T

talk to / about 16
tell 29
tenses
   future 11, 12
   passive 26
   past continuous 5
   past continuous / past simple
     5
   past perfect 10
   past simple 4, 8
     Table D, Table E
   past simple / past perfect 10
   past simple / present perfect 8
   present continuous 2, 3, 12
   present perfect continuous 9
   present perfect 6, 7, 8
   present simple 1, 3
     Table B
   present simple / present
     continuous 3
that
   in relative clauses 44
   in reported speech 29
the 30
themselves 31
think
   I think / don't think + should
     24
through 42
time
   conjunctions 14
   word order 18
to
   + infinitive 28
   preposition 42
too
   I . . . too 15
   too much / many 38
try 28

U

uncountable nouns 20, 30, 37,
   38
under 42
until 14, 20
up 42

V

verbs
+ direct/indirect objects 32
future 11, 12
+ infinitive 28
irregular 4, Table E
modals 22, 23, 24, 25, 28
passive 26
past participles 6, 7, 10, 26,
  Table D, Table E
past tenses 4, 5, 8, 10
present perfect tenses 6, 7, 8,
  9
present tenses 1, 2, 3, 12,
  14, Table B
+ prepositions 16
regular 4, 6, Table D
+ **to** + infinitive 28
word order 18
very 41

W

wait for 16
want 28
well 40, Table G
what? 19
when
  + past continuous 5
  + past perfect 10
  + present perfect 14
  + present simple 14
which 44
while 5
who 44
who? 19
will 11, 13
with 43
without 43
word order 18
worse 36, Table F
would 29
would like 27

Y

years old 20
yet 7
yourself/yourselves 31

Z

zero conditional 13